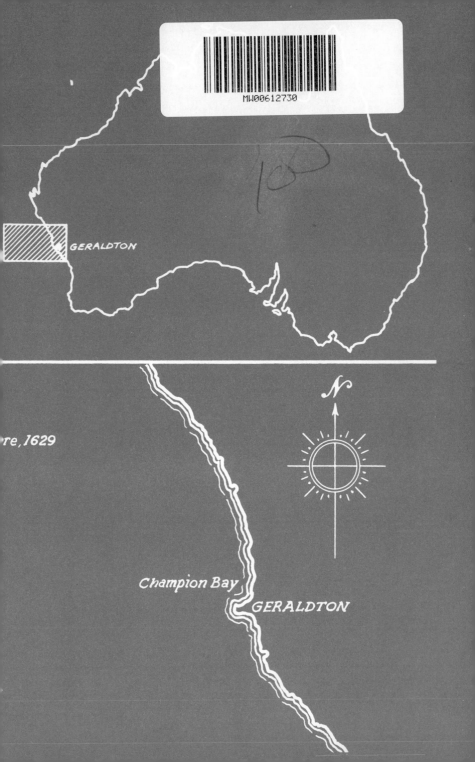

GERALDTON

re, 1629

Champion Bay

GERALDTON

N

THE WRECK
ON THE
HALF-MOON
REEF

Also by Hugh Edwards
GODS & LITTLE FISHES

ISLANDS OF ANGRY GHOSTS

THE WRECK ON THE HALF-MOON REEF

Hugh Edwards

Charles Scribner's Sons
New York

1 3 5 7 9 11 13 15 17 19 C/C 20 18 16 14 12 10 8 6 4 2

Printed in the United States of America
Library of Congress Catalog Card Number 73-5180
SBN 684-13550-7 (cloth)

To Maurice Glazier and
Muriel Thomas of the
Southern Abrolhos

ACKNOWLEDGMENTS

The writing of this book was made possible by the granting of a twelve month literary fellowship in 1968 by the Commonwealth Literary Fund. My gratitude is expressed in the way that the members of the Fund committee would wish it—between these covers.

I also wish to thank Muriel Thomas and Maurice Glazier of the Southern Abrolhos, and hope that the dedication of the book to them is some small acknowledgement of the great debt I owe them for hospitality and help in the Abrolhos over many years. The notes for this book were put together in their crayfish season shack, on Post Office Island, and their anchorage lagoon was the base for diving discovery work on the wreck of the *Zeewyk*.

Similarly I owe thanks to Frank Bombara, Syd Liddon, the Travia family and the Boschetti brothers, also fishing the Southern islands, and to the co-operative group which owns the crayfish carrier boat *Southern Lady*.

Divers Jack Sue, Dale Walsh, Geoff Clements, Neil McLaghlan, Tom Brady, and especially Max Cramer, played parts in the various phases of discovery of the wreck.

International Marine provided the Mercury motors used on our diving boats, and since 1968 Bob Ford has done more than could be required of any General Manager in keeping our engines running, despite rough handling among coral reefs and constant abuse in conditions of maximum sand and salt.

As a historical work the book required a great deal of research. In the Netherlands, B. C. W. Lap, assistant curator of the Maritiem Museum Prins Hendrik, in Rotterdam, arranged the illustrations of the *Padmos/Blydorp* ship model and references on ship design. Mrs M. A. P. Meilink-Roelofsz, the Keeper of the first section of the Algemeen Rijksarchief at S'Gravenhage organized the translation of the *Zeewyk* papers, and the research work was carried out by W. Wichard Timmers, of The Hague. Mr C. de Heer, of the University of Western Australia, made the translation of the *Zeewyk* journals supplied by B. Goppel, of Rotterdam, for the original *Zeewyk* expedition in 1963 sponsored by the West Australian Newspapers Pty. Ltd.

The Western Australian Museum Board, through its chairman, Sir Thomas Meagher, and museum director, W. D. L. Ride, supplied a substantial sum for *Zeewyk* work in 1968 and arranged translation of further papers in 1969. Mr. W. R. Cumming, secretary of the Commonwealth Literary Fund, Mr H. L. White, National Librarian at Canberra, and Miss Mollie Lukis, of the Battye Library in Western Australia, were extremely helpful. Professor G. C. Bolton of the Western Australian University History Department, provided interest and encouragement. Mrs Jeanette Atkinson typed the manuscript with patience and good humour, and Ansett Airlines assisted with travel grants for research.

Finally I owe a special debt to Dr P. E. Playford who did the early important research work on the *Zuytdorp* and Western Australian VOC wrecks; to Mr S. J. Wilson, who advised on pieces-of-eight and coinage, and to the late Henrietta Drake-Brockman, who wrote the monumental historical work *Voyage to Disaster* on the *Batavia* wreck, and gave personal impetus and encouragement to the present book.

To these people and many more who helped, some unknowingly, my grateful thanks.

Hugh Edwards

CONTENTS

ILLUSTRATIONS

1
The Tusk

In 1727 THE 38-GUN DUTCH EAST INDIA COMPANY SHIP *Zeewyk* was wrecked on a reef of the Abrolhos Islands off the Western Australian coast.

If she had been a mere two miles further north on her course, after 6,000 miles of sailing across the Indian Ocean from the Cape of Good Hope, she would have cleared the reef and sailed by, unknowing in the dark.

Or if she had been two hours faster on her seven month voyage from Europe, the lookouts would have sighted the surf before daylight faded, and shouted a warning in time to save the ship.

But the darkness fell early on that winter's evening, with scudding rain showers, and a low dark sky. The reef was waiting in the dusk, its outlying rocks concealed beneath a swollen and discoloured sea. The ship's bones and coral-grown cannon lie there yet.

On another blustery day in 1966, 239 years after the *Zeewyk* broached broken-masted in the agony of her shipwreck, I found a tusk spilled from the wreck.

It was lying in about four feet of water, inside the corals of the thirteen-mile shoal which Jan Steyns in 1727 called the Half-Moon Reef. The ivory was broken at the base, pitted by sea urchins, and raddled with the tunnels of marine worms. A forlorn relic of former glory, but still recognizable as the tusk of an elephant which once trumpeted on the plains of Africa half a world away.

The tusk was so similar to the fragments of dead sea-washed coral lying all around on the bottom that it could not have been more effectively camouflaged. It would have been easy to pass it by and perhaps I would have swum on but for the fact that in 1963 we spent weeks pulling similar tusks and pieces-of-eight out of a 1656 wreck called the *Vergulde Draeck*, 150 miles south at Cape Leschenault.

The curve of the battered shape was familiar, if unexpected, and excitement grabbed hard at a wreck diver's stomach. It was the sure sign of an old shipwreck close at hand, and for a crazy moment I wanted to take out my snorkel and shout in triumph to the waves and wondering sea-birds. The moment passed, and wry laughter followed.

The irony of it!

We had combed this reef in past years, searching for the main body of a wreck we knew must be there, but which we could never locate among the breakers and the corals. Days of looking under submarine ledges past the waving orange antennae of crayfish, and the flickering shapes of fish. Always hoping for the glint of brass, the white patina of lead, the worm-hollowed timbers that might mean a wreck. We burnt money, fuel, and precious time, but not a single trace of the ship could we find.

Of course it had to be there somewhere, but too much failure makes for a weariness of spirit. In 1966 we decided to forget the intensity and frustrations of wreck-hunting for a while, and to just go on fishing. And so without a search, without a plan, I stumbled on the tusk which pointed to the wreck on the Half-Moon reef.

The reef stretched from horizon to horizon, its top a massive plateau of dead coral, cratered and pitted like the moon. A bastion 400 yards wide in some places. The outside

2

rim was littered with boulders and solid blocks of coral torn loose and flung up by the waves. Westwards lay the dark blue of deep water—league after league of Indian Ocean stretching away without another rock or scrap of dry land between the reef and Africa.

We had not intended diving there that day. We had been jewfishing and running a set-line for sharks down at Pelsaert Island ten miles to the south. But a spiteful wind rose overnight, and by morning whitecaps were scudding across the lagoon. The south-easter set the crayfishing boats shouldering and jostling at their jetties, and there were high rows of creaming white breakers behind Pelsaert Island. Diving there was clearly impossible.

With the wind from that quarter the only likely sheltered water lay to the west, inside the reef which *Zeewyk* skipper Jan Steyns named long ago from its shape like a horned half-moon. It was twelve miles of travel, keel-jolting from one wave to the next in the de Havilland aluminium dory. Even above the angry-wasp noise of the forty horsepower Evinrude outboard motor we heard the sound of the reef long before we reached it. Huge green swells were piling and breaking on the western skyline, the muffled booming of the breakers drifting to us down the wind sounding like the guns of a ghost ship from long ago.

On the ocean side the backwash seethed and frothed like a giant's cauldron. But inside, in the lagoon, the green shallows were wind-ruffled but calm and clear.

I threw the anchor out near a patch of yellow coral lumps without taking much notice of where we were. One mile of the reef was much the same as the next and there were fish in all the lumps. The anchor fell with a splash and a rattle of chain. Dale Walsh and Jack Sue, who had their diving gear on, were quickly over the side. I waited a little longer to let the anchor bite and make sure it was holding before following them, then slid below the silver skin of the surface in the usual cloud of bubbles of entry. As I loaded my speargun I looked down and saw with astonishment the curve of the ivory.

It lay in the middle of a saucer-shaped depression of sand,

3

with waving beards and strands of seaweed growing around and masking it from sight from more than a few yards away in any direction. The odds against swimming over this one spot in all the miles of green water along the reef were so tremendous that for a long time I had the feeling I must have dreamed it all. I had to feel the worm-hollowed weight of the ivory in my hands, caress the eroded surface, for reassurance.

We like to feel we are masters of our fates, and plan our lives to paths and patterns, years ahead. It is a little frightening when blind chance intervenes, capriciously swinging the whole course of our existence around the compass, and sometimes changing things so that our personal worlds are never the same again. The chance discovery of the tusk changed my own life in such a way. On the seaworn peg of the ivory hangs my tale. . . .

2
The *Zeewyk*

It was not intended that Jan Steyns should skipper the new ship *Zeewyk* to the Indies when the Dutch East India Company autumn fleet sailed in 1726.

The directors of the Chamber of Zeeland, meeting to select their officers on 19 August 1726, first chose Jan Bogaard for the *Zeewyk* because of his steadiness and experience. But on 5 September, the directors—dressed in the sober dark woollen garments and tall black hats of their time—reconsidered, and recorded in the minutes of that day's meeting: "Because of the disease and indisposition of Jan Bogaard to appoint as skipper of the ship *Zeewyk*, Jan Steyns of Middelburg."

And so it was done.

Whether Bogaard's chagrined loss stemmed from a recurrence of malaria or dysentery from the tropics, or the debilitating effects of scurvy or one of the other shipboard curses, we do not know. But the ailment which took the *Zeewyk* from him and gave her to Steyns altered history.

The ship was the newest and finest of the Indies fleet.

A 145 feet East Indiaman, with thirty-eight guns and 200 men, her poop was magnificent in green paint and gold gilt. The red lion figurehead of the sea province of Zeeland snarled at her prow, and streamers and forked forty-foot pennants flew from her mastheads. She was so new that the lice and black rats and blood-sucking bugs, which infested every ship of the time, had not yet moved in and only the clean wood-chips of shipwrights were to be found in the bilges.

Steyns was the uppersteersman (first mate) of the ship *Heinkenssand*, and the *Zeewyk* was to be his first command. Probably, with his wife Elisabet de Volder and their friends, he would have celebrated his good fortune on that night of 5 September 1726, in the way traditional among the Dutch middle class on such important occasions. The tables groaning with good food and brandy, Spanish wines, and Dutch and German beer flowing with frequent toasts to the host's health and future happiness.

It is likely that they were not too sorrowful about the sickness of Jan Bogaard. There may even have been some jocular toasts to his indisposition as the evening wore on and the faces of the drinkers became flushed and fiery, and their speech and laughter louder. If you had told brandy-beaming Jan Steyns that night that he would become a famous skipper, remembered centuries after his contemporaries had been forgotten, he would have believed it in the general mood of elation and congratulation.

But it is unlikely that he would have chosen the fame for which he was destined, if he had been given the choice that evening. Better by far to have remained the mate of the *Heinkenssand*. . . .

New ship and new skipper were to sail together to ruin at the end of the world, their story of tangled fates to achieve a place in history. The guns of the *Zeewyk* still lie today in the wash of the surf of a coral reef of the Albrolhos Islands on the far side of the blue Indian Ocean, and her name lives on in the Zeewyk Channel on the Admiralty charts. The name Steyns is nowhere to be found, except in the trial records of de Vereenigde Oost-Indische Compagnie, the great

6

Dutch United East India Company, and among the sentences pronounced on criminals in Batavia in the year 1729.

But mercifully men cannot see into the future. In 1726 Jan Steyns was the envy of every officer in the Zeeland fleet. The command of an Indiaman of the first class, such as the *Zeewyk*, was the ultimate dream of all of them. For most it would remain a dream because top commands were rare and not easily come by. Only two of the largest class of Indiamen were completed in all the Netherlands in 1726, and the *Zeewyk* was the vessel added to the Zeeland fleet. Even though Steyns was a second choice, the honour of gaining the command of such a ship must have taken his breath away. It was the most momentous event in his seafaring career. Coupled with the joy would have been the sobering knowledge of the enormous responsibility involved in the trust of such a huge and magnificent vessel and so large a company of men, on the longest regular sea route in the known world.

These things make his decision in the Indian Ocean half-a-year later the more difficult to understand.

For the Dutch East India Company was such a huge and powerful organization that even skippers were merely humble servants, and it was implacable in its wrath towards those who disobeyed its orders. A man who lost a ship by wilfully disregarding the sailing instructions stood to forfeit his rank, his worldly possessions, his name, honour, and perhaps even his life. There was no escape from its cold justice other than as a hunted fugitive, or in exile.

The Vereenigde Oost-Indische Compagnie was the most powerful single commercial concern the world has ever known. General Motors, British Tobacco, Ford, The Shell Company, Mitsubishi, Standard Oil—any of the other giant holdings of today are on the level of village bootmakers compared with the might and power and influence once wielded by the VOC.

It was richer and stronger than many nations of its time. In 1726 it had more than 200 ships, 30,000 soldiers, sailors, and servants, and a monopoly of all trade in a dominion encompassing a quarter of the world. Its trading empire stretched across an area reaching from the Cape of Good Hope to India, Ceylon, Sumatra, Java, the Celebes and Spice Islands, and the ports of Malaya, China and Japan. The Company was authorized by the home government of the Netherlands to make war or trade, to build cities, forts, or factories. It appointed its own magistrates and ministers of religion. It held the power of life and death over its own servants and over millions of Asiatics, and sometimes sent ships and armies to crush native potentates who would not meet its trade demands.

The famed and feared initials VOC were stamped into cannon butts, sword hilts, factory gates, ships' beams, compass rims, and the silver candlesticks and knife handles on the governor's table at Batavia. They were better known, some complained, than the Holy Cross of the church.

But the complaints were not too loud. Most of the men of influence in Holland were shareholders in the wealth. In Amsterdam, home of the richest of the six *Kamers* or Chambers which made up the united company, there was a saying that, "Jesus Christ is good, but trade is better!"

It was also said that the Dutch had two gods and that the Guilder prevailed on earth. When Steyns and the *Zeewyk* sailed for the East Indies at the end of 1726 it seemed that the prosperity of the Company could never end.

In fact corruption was already prevalent; the white ants undermining the foundations. But the thunder of the mighty fall would not be heard for half-a-century yet.

. . So far as the monied middle-class of the Netherlands, who comprised the bulk of the shareholders, were concerned, the dividends in six successive years from 1715 to 1720 had been forty per cent. They were still high in 1726 and there was no reason to believe, as the Company recruiting officers began signing on crew for the *Zeewyk*, that they might not rise again to greater heights.

The stolid burghers of the Chamber of the sea province of Zeeland, which appointed Jan Steyns and fitted out the *Zeewyk* for the Indies, could be excused a strong sense of self-satisfaction as they puffed on their long clay pipes in conclave and reviewed their trading figures.

8

The success of the Dutch East India Company was watched with malice abroad. Other nations claimed that Netherlanders were stubborn, complacent, with a built-in belief that they were right in all things. "Pig-headed Hollanders" the English called them.

But the Dutch were more practical than sensitive, and could afford to ignore such remarks. At the time Steyns received his commission they were enjoying a period of unparalleled national prosperity. If success was the criterion, then their judgment was right more often than their rivals, at least in the spheres of trade and commerce.

Merchant ships flying the red-white-and-blue flag of Holland carried the bulk of the cargoes in European waters. Baltic grain, Norwegian timber, Portuguese salt and olives, Italian and Spanish wine, English iron and copperware, Dutch beer and cheeses—and the huge redistribution of spices and exotic goods from the East which arrived in Netherlands ports in the holds of every homeward bound East Indiaman.

They had the biggest herring, whaling, and cod fleets, sailing on the North Sea and in Greenland and Atlantic waters. The rich stink of salt herring, drying cod fish, and whale oil hung over every fishing hamlet in Holland. Barges carried cargo of all descriptions up the great rivers into the very centre of Europe, and brought other goods back for re-sale and re-shipping abroad.

Magnificent Amsterdam was the banking and business hub of the world. Dutch freight rates were the lowest, their insurance terms were the best, and their loans were made on the most reasonable conditions. The resentment and envy of their competitors was understandable.

Dutch stubbornness, particularly in adversity, was a national trait. It stemmed from the dour tenacity of ancestors who had to struggle for mere survival in a hostile environment which in Roman times was a chain of swamps and marshes; the waterlogged junction where the great rivers Rhine, Maas, and Schelde emptied the waters of central Europe into a vast sink, backing the dune frontage of the North Sea. A wet, wind-swept wilderness.

No-one knows who built the first platform for a house, or the first wicker dyke to hold back the floods—any more than we know now who built the first wheel or the first boat. But by steady toil the Dutch turned their watery wasteland into green fields and plump prosperity by the 1600s and 1700s. There was a saying: "God made the world, but the Dutch made Holland." In 1726 windmills clanked their pumps beside canals running straight mile after mile and thronged with barge traffic. On every horizon there were red-bricked towns with well-to-do houses. There were great engineering works—formidable dykes holding back the turbulent North Sea, which fretted behind the dunes.

The desolate marshes were drained by windmill operated pumps and made into fields for dairy cattle. There was the visible miracle of whole towns, such as Amsterdam, built on piles and reclaimed land. Ports where the masts of shipping spiked the sky, as thick as forests.

It was a land of culture as well as commerce, where painters such as Rubens, Rembrandt, Vermeer, Van Dyke, Jan Steen, Heronimus Bosch, Pieter de Hooch, Janssens, Van der Hyden, Van de Velde, van Goyen, and others produced canvases which endured centuries after their own time.

It was a land of ostentatious cleanliness where every Dutch housewife scrubbed and rubbed her floors daily and even washed the doorstep and pavement of the street outside. There was charity, with hospitals, poorhouses, and institutions unmatched by any other country in Europe. The Netherlands were stolidly democratic with the majority of affairs—whether business, politics, or the running of a city— in the hands of elected committees. There was a tolerance to unorthodox belief which made Holland a haven for poor hunted refugees, sought for their lives in other parts of a Europe where bloody bigotry and persecution were the rules rather than the exceptions. Portuguese and Spanish, Jews, French Hugenots, English Quakers, and the Pilgrim Fathers, gratefully took shelter in turn.

The Netherlanders were also merry folk, though even their enjoyment was touched by the national energy and seriousness of purpose. Their winter sport was ice-skating, and racers sometimes travelled more than 100 miles in a day over frozen canals, estuaries, and the Zuider Zee. They had *kermises*, or fairs, which went on for a fortnight at a time, with dancing and singing in the streets. They drank a formidable amount of beer, wine, and spirits, and at civic banquets there were sometimes as many as fifty full-glass toasts. Wine was served in taverns in pewter pitchers ranging from two pint to gallon-and-a-half capacity. Women drank as heavily as the men.

"Our nation must drink or die!" declared Governor Jan Pieterszoon Coen at Batavia in the Indies in the 1620s. A statement of popular sentiment often quoted in after years.

A rich, merry, healthy, and humanitarian nation—God be thanked and praised, as the burghers might have said.

And if this sounds too good to be true, too eulogistic, there was also a dark side to the picture. The Dutch, tolerant at home, were ruthless and oppressive colonists abroad. They sought monopolies of trade throughout the East, manipulating prices to their own requirements and enforcing their will with the sword. The entire population of the Spice Islands of Banda was slaughtered in 1621, and the homes and villages razed, for breach of a trade treaty.

In this kind of harshness they did not stand alone. The English, a nation notable in history for social conscience and a sense of fair play, carried away millions of negroes from West Africa as slaves to be sold into bondage in the Americas. A loathsome trade of blood, death, and iniquity which stank as much as the slavers' ships. The Spaniards reduced the population of Mexico from 11 million in 1519 to $2\frac{1}{2}$ million in 1597 by the sword, sickness, and brutal forced labour in mines and plantations. The Portuguese cut noses and hands off Moorish prisoners.

Though the Dutch permitted unusual freedom of con-science for the times in matters of religion, politics, and association between the sexes, common law was harsh indeed. The Dutch were unforgiving with wrongdoers.

Outside every gate of every major town in Holland stood the black silhouettes of public gibbets.

11

There were varied offences for which a man or woman's life could be forfeit. They ranged from murder to witchcraft, mutiny, embezzlement, stealing bodies for surgeons' anatomy classes or sorcery, counterfeiting, forgery and arson, and major theft.

Criminals could be beheaded or broken on the wheel for especially serious offences, or garrotted in the Spanish style. But the most usual capital punishment was hanging. The gibbets or gallows were commonly about fifteen feet high and wide enough to take six or more of the condemned.

Sometimes, like the *Batavia* mutineers on the Australian coast in 1629, malefactors had hands chopped off at the wrist before being hanged. Others were burned with a brand, or mutilated by cutting, before execution. Torture was legal when authorized by a magistrate, either as a punishment or to extract confession from a suspect. The rack, hot irons, the boot, pincers, the water cure, were old favourites.

Petty thieves had ears cut off, or their hands or faces hot-branded with a letter which scarred and stamped them for life. Persistent pilfering could mean the loss of a hand or the gallows. Flogging was frequently administered, especially in the services and aboard ship.

The Amsterdam hangman, who earned three guilders for a beheading (with nine guilders bonus if he buried the corpse), three guilders a stroke for breaking on the wheel, or a flogging, executed 209 death sentences in the last three months of 1699. He was well paid. A common seaman of the India Company earned little more than ten guilders a month, though his keep and uniform were supplied. A VOC merchant such as Jan Nebbens, serving in the Indies, earned twenty-four guilders a month; an Indiaman skipper, such as Steyns, forty-eight guilders a month.

Punishments were often made to fit the crime, especially on board ship. A thief would have his hand nailed to the mast and be left to tear it free in his own good time. A murderer could be bound face to face with the body of his victim and thrown overboard. Homosexuals were sometimes treated the same way.

At least by 1727 they were no longer burning witches, and the more horrific capital punishments were less commonly used. But, as we shall see with the men of the *Zeewyk*, vengeful brutality was still the chief instrument of justice.

Superstition, as elsewhere in Europe, was rife. People still half-believed in witches and warlocks. A favourite charm to ward off fever or evil was a nut-shell full of spider's heads hung on the chest. If you were fussy about spiders, a verse from the Bible would do.

A disgusting but immensely popular salve was froth from soaping the head of a hanged man or someone who had died violently, mixed with human blood, linseed, and spices. All sorts of grisly relics from executions were much in demand. Relatives of an executed criminal often had to fight to keep the corpse intact.

It was an age abysmally ignorant in matters of medicine, hygiene, and cleanliness. Plagues and epidemics were believed to be entirely the result of the wrath of God.

No one washed very often, though women scrubbed their floors daily. A hip-bath once a week for their bodies was regarded as being rather unnecessarily fastidious. The fine ladies and gentlemen of the time must have reeked muskily under their splendid garments. The poor, of course, didn't wash at all, and stank. Canals were used as drains and sewers, and epidemics carried off huge numbers of people living in dirt and squalor.

But the same could be said of any country in Europe. Criminal punishments were universally savage. Plagues took rich and poor alike. Knowledge in medical matters was little advanced from the Middle Ages. Holland was as good a place as any and considerably better than most. Jan Steyns and his officers most likely thought their country a model of cleanliness, justice, and good health, and by the standards of their time they were no doubt right.

It is interesting that the *Zeewyk* was divided from the first great wave of exploration of the world by sea—Columbus, Dias, da Gama, Magellan—by the same period of about 250 years as separates Jan Steyns and his men from our own time.

The East Indiamen sailors would doubtless have considered Columbus' ships primitive. Perhaps they would have been amused at the sailing rig, the stubby, bell-mouthed cannon, and the ponderous navigating astrolabes. But there was not such a wide gap between them. Columbus' or Magellan's men could have sailed the *Zeewyk*, and the *Zeewyk* crew could have fitted in comfortably aboard Nelson's flagship *Victory*. But none of the sailors of any of those crews, from Columbus in 1492 to Nelson in 1805, would find anything familiar aboard a modern merchantman or man o' war. On a ship of the 1960s they would be able to distinguish the bow, the stern, the wheel, and the ship's bell. Everything else has changed.

In Jan Steyns' day it took an East Indiaman like the *Zeewyk* anything from five to nine months to sail from her home Netherlands port and reach Batavia in the East Indies. Often, it took two years for a letter to reach its destination and a reply to be received, and men could be dead for months before the news reached their relatives and loved ones in Holland. Today a jet airliner bridges the distance in a matter of hours, and from Djakarta most places in the world can be reached within minutes of picking up the telephone.

Every century has its dark corners . Better to look for the brightness, the good, which exists in every age. There were very many happy qualities in the Holland of Jan Steyns' time. Perhaps the most admirable of the Dutch characteristics was the way in which Netherlanders were able to work together for common benefit. It may have been a legacy from the days when everyone in a town or village toiled together to mend the dykes. But no other nation found the same willingness to work in council and on committees, nor rivalled the Dutch success of commerce on a co-operative basis. Where trade in other countries in the 1700s was usually in the hands of individual merchants or family cartels, Dutch enterprise was invariably shared to a code of well-defined and equitable rules.

Banks, insurance, money-lending, trading concerns, even the little coastal ships plying to the Baltic and Mediterranean, were jointly owned by a varying number of shareholders.

14

While profits were divided and spread, the distribution was more even than in other countries and there was more solidarity and continuity in business. The endorsement of Dutch good sense is that many of the business systems which they developed two and three centuries ago are universal practice throughout the world today.

The most successful of all the Dutch companies was the splendid Vereenigde Oost-Indische Compagnie. The United East India Company. It was founded in 1602 and was probably the greatest example of the Dutch ability to sink selfish individual interests and pull together for the common cause.

When Netherlands ships first began trading to the East in the 1590s, after the sea-power of Spain and Portugal had been broken by English gunfire and God's storm in the débâcle of the Armada, private cartels and companies from every sea province in Holland sent ships into the Indian Ocean. These merchant-adventurers competed with each other, often fiercely, for the spices of the eastern seas.

The rajahs and sultans who had sulkily sold to a Portuguese monopoly for more than a century, were delighted. They played off one Dutchman against another, and bargained with the English against them both. Prices rose out of all proportion and there was general ill-feeling. Clearly the situation could not continue.

The Dutch had always organized their commerce with tight-purse shrewdness. Apart from the annoyance of paying more than a product was worth, there was also a problem of protection of merchant ships. The resentful remnants of Portuguese shipping strength still kept the seas and the English interlopers showed truculence which seemed likely to develop into open hostility at any time.

A unified front was the answer, both for trade and protection. A Dutch fleet would be impregnable where single ships were vulnerable.

In 1602 the merchant towns of Amsterdam, Rotterdam, Zeeland, Delft, Enkhuisen, and Hoorn, which had formed independent companies to send ships sailing on the Indies trade, agreed to sink their provincial jealousies. They banded together as De Vereenigde Oost-Indische Compagnie, with elected directors in proportion to the wealth of the provinces, and shareholders from all over the Netherlands.

The combine was so successful that within twenty years it had completely eliminated its Portuguese and English competitors. By cannon fire, shrewd trade treaties, and the unremitting hard work of its servants it came to dominate the entire Eastern world. In 1726 it was the most powerful trading concern the world had ever known, an empire in its own right. It was the pride of the Netherlands nation, and of its servants such as skipper Jan Steyns of Middelburg.

In September, 1726, the *Zeewyk* signed on her crew. In true seafaring tradition they were a mixed bag. Many of them, red-eyed and suffering from a gross surfeit of grog, were the ironically-christened *Heeren zes Weken*, Lords of Six Weeks, or *Heeren varen gasten*, Gentlemen Voyagers. They were men who had finished a three year term of service with the Company not long before, and had spent all their accumulated back-pay in a glorious running debauch between the taverns and the generous-fleshed harlots of the ports. Now they were once again penniless and destitute and looking for a job on a ship. It was the only life known to the old hands; hardened reprobates with Chinese tattoos and scurvy-gapped teeth, and the tan of the tropics still on their sallow faces and leather necks. They chewed tobacco, spitting with long and accurate jets. Using Malay and Indian oaths they talked in a familiar East Indiaman fo'c'sle slang, and told outrageous yarns to people who had never left Holland of strange ports and stranger customs in lands where the Ten Commandments were unknown. Some of the strangest stories were true.

Many of the recruits were fresh-faced country boys lured by romantic tales of the tropics. The old hands eyed them with veiled amusement. Others were sharp-eyed clerks signing on for the main chance of making money on the side—double-dealing on the fringes of Company business, as many had done before them.

And there were the professionals, the senior seamen, petty

16

officers and mates, strong-armed, clear-eyed, competent men. They were the backbone of the Company's fleet, and they had been bred to the sea and her moods from boyhood. Men with rope-hard hands and a roll to their gait. Though the real seamen were a minority on any ship, perhaps less than a quarter, they would mould the old work-dodgers, the wet-nosed boys, and the smart clerks into the semblance of a working crew, whether they liked it or not. It was believed that the thump of a fist, the sting of a rope's end, or the leathern whistle of the lash, were the only language understood by the rabble of the fo'c'sle.

There was no privilege system in the fleet. Men gained advancement by skill, diligence, and good example. Many skippers and admirals had risen from the ranks, and even the most sought after post of all, the office of governor at Batavia, was open to any man.

Governor-General J. P. Coen, the first governor at Batavia and the architect of the Indies empire, sailed out from Holland as a clerk before achieving his greatness. Antonie van Diemen, his celebrated protégé, enlisted as a bankrupt under an assumed name and triumphed over his difficulties to become Governor from 1636-45. A sea-cook, Francis Caron, rose above salt pork and ships'-biscuit to become Director General in 1645-50. Jacob Mossel (1750-61) and Reinier de Klerk (1777-80) originally enlisted as common seamen and came from the scurvy quarters 'tween decks on Indiamen as the first step on the way to becoming distinguished Governors.

Like the Foreign Legion of our own century, men joining the VOC were judged on what they were, not what they had been. Often able and qualified men enlisted in lowly positions simply to get away from Holland. Trouble with a woman, gambling debts, a social disgrace . . . or just boredom with routine. The reasons were as varied as human nature.

The men of the *Zeewyk* were enrolled on a cold foggy morning at the Company courtyard in Middelburg, the main town of the sea province of Zeeland. Enrolment day was announced at dawn by trumpets and drums and a shouting, protesting, struggling mass of would-be sailors,

17

soldiers and Company servants jamming the cobbled street outside the gates, and jostling for the chance to put their signatures to a contract. For winter was coming on, and a poor man could starve to death in snow-bound streets. Common hands signed on for three or five years. The skipper and commissioned officers signed for five years and were spared the muddy struggle of enlistment day.

Signatures taken, their lives signed away for three years of Company service, the sailors and soldiers were issued with their kit and marched away to barracks. On a day at the end of September they were rowed out in barges to the ship, already provisioned for sea, which lay out in the roadstead. Once aboard the roll was called, each man answering his name and being assigned to a watch. The Company's articles were read, with the usual promises of rewards for honest and arduous labour and threats of dire punishments for slackers or miscreants. As soon as they were dismissed the experienced hands ran to grab the best berths, while the new ones looked around bewildered. It was much like any other service, ancient or modern.

Soon enough, the *Zeewyk* was ready for sea. The officers, with firm authoritarian voices, walked the quarter deck, magnificent in their blue and red formal uniforms. The boatswains and petty officers relayed the orders, bellowing in coarser tones to the common hands. The capstans turned, and the great fluked anchors were dragged up out of the mud of the Schelde estuary and were secured and lashed, dripping, to the catheads projecting from her bows. The warps from the small towing vessels tightened and the great ship began to move.

The voyage had begun.

3
Silver and Spices

OF THE 208 SEAMEN AND SOLDIERS WHO TOOK THEIR KIT TO the quayside to sail aboard the East Indiaman *Zeewyk* on that autumn day of 1726, only one man in three would ever see Holland again.

This was a higher mortality than the usual because it was to be an extraordinary voyage. But the deaths, the diseases, the crippling accidents of a seafaring life in those times, were taken for granted.

The English admiral Anson sailed down Channel in 1743 with six ships and 2,000 British seamen. His expedition hoped to repeat the legendary exploits of Francis Drake, the scourge of the Spaniards 140 years before, by harrying shipping and sacking Spanish colonial towns on the Pacific coast of South America.

A year later Anson was cruising almost despairingly near the Philippines. 1,300 of his sailors were dead from sickness, the ships he had captured were abandoned because he did not have the men to crew them, and his flag-ship *Centurion* was left with only enough hands to man one gun in two.

Yet his expedition was to be accounted a success. The huge Spanish galleon *Nuestra Senora de Covadonga*, awaited as the last desperate gamble of the voyage, sailed into his path on a sunlit day, and the grateful Britishers fought so hard and well that they captured her in ninety minutes. They lost only two dead and seventeen wounded in the action, and it took thirty-two wagons to carry the treasure when they returned to London.

Though the cost in men on the voyage was terrible, any seaman of the time would have declared the result well worth it, and shrugged at the scurvy mortality. A man could not expect to live forever.

Deaths, both on ship and shore, reached appalling heights in voyaging to the Indies, from Magellan's time—only a third of his crews survived the circumnavigation of the world—to Nelson's day, three centuries later.

Though the first feelings of the Spanish and Portuguese discoverers of the Indies were joy at the wealth, the harvest was to be bitter-sweet, as the Dutch discovered after them.

The tropics exacted grim tribute in return for the chests of gold and silver, the bales of spices taken. A toll marked by grey gravestones in rows and the splashes of seamen's bodies dropped overside into equatorial blue waters.

While the Armada defeat of 1588 was the most humiliating and costly reversal of arms in the history of Spain and Portugal—so much so that Phillip II thought God had turned against him—the men and ships lost in that costly débâcle were nothing compared with the vessels wrecked, sunk, and captured, the men dead of wars and disease, in the years of Indies colonization.

From a half to one third of the crews commonly died from sickness on long voyages. Many of those who survived became listless and enervated from recurrent illness or the oppressive climate. They served out their time with little heart, so that when Drake and the cutlass-swinging English buccaneers, bounding with energy and courage, swooped on garrisons and armies of New World Spaniards they conquered them as ridiculously easily as Cortez and Pizarro's men had stampeded Aztec and Inca legions in their hundred

20

thousands, only fifty years before. The tropics sapped men's strength and will.

There is no denying that the wealth won from the East and West Indies was dazzling. Mexico alone was to supply half the world's silver. But the upkeep of colonial forts and garrisons, the cost of building and sailing the ships, was stupendous in proportion. The cost in lives—all too often the bravest and the best—was enormous. And during the sixteenth and seventeenth centuries Spain became involved in a series of European wars of dogma and religion which further sucked her strength.

There could almost have been a curse on the gold and silver grabbed and gouged from the earth of the new territories. Ironically the Protestant countries, the enemies of Spain and Portugal, filched a great deal of it by under-cover trade and by private loans to inefficient and corrupt Cadiz and Lisbon merchants.

The Dutch, in particular, had a prosperous trade through Spain's back door, the Portuguese port of Lisbon, for salt, olives, wines, and the spices which all Europe demanded. There was really no reason why the Dutch should want to go to the Indies themselves at all.

But in 1580 the crowns of Spain and Portugal were united under the cold-steel hand of Protestantism's implacable foe, Phillip II of Spain. The port of Lisbon was closed. The door slammed shut. For Northern Europeans the supply of spices and pieces of eight was stopped—except for those that the buccaneers took without the King of Spain's permission, purchased by cannon and cutlass, receipted in blood.

The situation became intolerable for both sides, and was one of the reasons for the despatch of the Armada in 1588. Its defeat was a crushing blow to Portugal, the poor relation of the alliance. She lost her capital ships, and her status as a sea power. She was long weakened by the years, the voyages, the fevers, the crushing colonial costs. For limping Portugal the Armada was the breaking of the crutch, and the way was laid open to the East Indies for the Dutch and English to sail for their own spices.

The Dutch East India Company, by virtue of Dutch

determination and force of action, became heir-apparent to the eastern seas.

The Dutch, fair-haired, blue-eyed, and rosy-cheeked, brought a new energy and ruthlessness of purpose to the East. Native princes who had supported them against the Portuguese in the belief that anything was better than the former oppression, found to their sorrow that the Dutch were quite as cruel and infinitely more efficient.

The early Netherlanders in the East pursued their trade with almost religious zeal. They spoke of their Company, its aims and ideals, in the way in which other men cherished a religion. Their Mecca, the Holy city, was Batavia.

In 1618 it was a mud village bearing no resemblance to the stately white-walled colonial city where Jan Steyns and the *Zeewyk* survivors would make their sensational arrival in 1728. It was a cluster of bamboo huts behind palisades, backed by buffalo swamps and rice paddies, and cut through by fever rivers. But it had the advantage of lying close to Sunda Straits, the natural gateway from the Indian Ocean to the Spice Islands, and it appeared ideally located to command war and peace throughout the East. For this reason Governor Jan Pieterszoon Coen chose it to be the VOC central base of operations in the Indies, and despite the fact that its foetid climate was demonstrably unsuitable for Europeans—they died in hundreds year by year—it remained the Dutch capital for more than three centuries. Today it is Djakarta, capital of Indonesia.

The original name was Jacartra, but Dutchmen who withstood a siege by Javanese forces there in 1618 called it Batavia, after a legendary tribe of heroes in the Fatherland in Roman times.

They set about building their East Indies capital with characteristic energy. Forts, walls, long streets, canals with shady trees and Holland-style houses were built. The buildings had white-washed door-steps like those at home. The streets were cobbled with Dutch bricks. The gables of the houses and churches were Dutch, and so were the round red cheeses, the smoked cod and salt herring in barrels in the market stalls. In some streets, but for the oppressive heat, you could believe yourself in Amsterdam. Over all hung the spirit of the VOC.

From the security of the Batavia base lines of forts and factories were methodically established, reaching out to India, Ceylon, Japan, the Spice Islands, the Cape of Good Hope. A series of ruthless but commercially-brilliant early governors, of whom Jan Pieterszoon Coen and Antonie van Diemen were the greatest, created a trade empire without precedent.

Their first principle was monopoly and they enforced their credo mercilessly. Independent native trade in spices and monopoly goods was stamped out, and offending ships were sunk. The only trade permitted was that which went through the factories of the Dutch East India Company.

So the VOC grew and prospered, and spread its tentacles, and increased its wealth, until it seemed it must burst at the seams with golden returns. "The Golden Age" the Dutch called it at home in Holland, where the profits were distributed in joyous dividends. Through the 1600s a whole national way of living was changed by the spices and goods, silks, fans, and trinkets flashing, glittering, flooding in from the East. Thousands of Dutchmen were going out every year, or coming home again from service in the great Company. Each man was changed by his experience, and brought back a little of the atmosphere of the coconut coasts, the exotic bazaars, the tropic perfumes, the lush sensuality of the East.

By the time Jan Steyns received his command of the *Zeewyk* the Dutch had been sailing to the East Indies for 130 years, and he must have grown up in an atmosphere of ships and shipping, the teak scents and traditions of the Indies trade.

Much later, in the 1700s and 1800s, coffee and tea became the most important exports of the East, but spices were the first cargoes so eagerly sought by Europeans.

The original El Dorado, the dream and desire of both Columbus and Vasco da Gama, was the Spice Islands.

These were a small group of islands named the Moluccas, sitting astride the equator between the northern tip of New Guinea and the southern extremity of the Philippines. They were remarkable in that they were the only place in the world that produced cloves.

Spices, and particularly cloves, were regarded as an essential by Europeans of 400 years ago. The modern cook uses a pinch here and there to add piquancy to dishes. A finishing touch. But in Old Europe spices were used in bulk by the sack, as actual preservatives.

In the heavy snows of European winters, when the ground froze iron-hard, there was a chronic shortage of feed for sheep and cattle. Every autumn a few picked animals were selected for hand-feeding and breeding, and the rest were slaughtered and the carcasses hung and treated so that they would last the winter. Rough salting did the job, but it made the meat bitter to the palate. Spices, for those who could afford them, preserved better and added flavour. They disguised meat that was a little gamey or on the rank side.

The main spices were cloves, nutmeg, mace, and cinnamon. But the trade also took in ginger, sugar, myrrh, waxes, perfumes, unguents, and ointments. Rhubarb from China was much in demand as a medicine. There were also Chinese aphrodisiacs and love charms, silks from Japan, rubies from Tibet, sapphires from Ceylon, indigo and emeralds from India, as well as carved ivory, silver-work, cotton cloth, and pearls from the Red Sea and Persian Gulf.

Before 1500 the eastern end of the Spice Trade lay in the hands of Muslims: Arabs, Turks, and Moors. The goods were moved westwards through a series of bazaars from Malacca to India, and on again by Arab dhow and Indian baghla to the headwaters of the Red Sea and Persian Gulf. From there they went by jolting camel train across mountain and desert to the ancient markets of Cairo, Damascus, Aleppo, and Baghdad. There they were exchanged for European tin, copper, mirrors, glassware, leather, salt, weapons, and armour.

It was a rich and romantic trade, and supported a great deal of wealth and power in Asia and Europe. For centuries the Venetians and Genovese held the monopoly of the Mediterranean end, buying from the Muslims and selling to the rest of Europe. As middlemen, they and the Arabs and

Turks reaped fat-purse profits. Because the goods passed through so many hands the costs to the eventual customers were considerable.

Anyone who could cut out the middlemen and sail ships direct to the Indies sources of the trade—the term "Indies" at the time embraced all countries from Arabia to Japan and all natives who were not Negroes or Moors were called "Indians"—could buy at a fraction of the normal price and profit enormously on return to Europe.

There was another reason, too, why the western Europeans wanted to break the Mohammedan monopolies of the spice trade.

For centuries the princes of Christendom had been warring against the Mohammedans in fruitless crusades, trying to win back the birthplace of Christ from the accursed Saracen. Blood and tears, and broken banners, mingled in the dust of Middle Eastern battlefields. When force of arms failed the chagrined crusader strategists considered economic encirclement. The spice trade was known to be a most important source of wealth to the Turks, and to deny it to them would be a crippling blow. It was said that to defeat the Turk in battle was merely to singe his beard and the thick black hairs would grow again. But to cut his trade routes would be to lop a limb.

These were the twin motives. To reach the source of riches, and strike the Infidel. Bernal Diaz, the conquistador of Mexico, put it concisely: "To serve God and His Majesty, to give light to those who were in darkness, and to grow rich as all men wish to do." Wealth on earth and a secure place in Heaven afterward—what more, indeed, could a man desire.

Before 1400, Europeans did not have the ships or the navigational or geographical skill to make long ocean voyages. The Greek-Egyptian geographer, Ptolemy, was still universally accepted as the great authority though his teachings dated from 150 A.D. He had stated flatly that the Atlantic was un-navigable, and the Indian Ocean a land-locked sea. The Atlantic was called "The Green Sea of Darkness," and it was believed that ships venturing too far out on it risked being carried over the waterfall of the edge of the world. It was said that men venturing south towards the equator would turn black like Negroes, and if they persisted in their folly would eventually roast alive in the fierce rays of the sun.

But with the Renaissance came new knowledge in astronomy and mathematics which made navigation out of sight of land a practical possibility. Ships improved with the experience of new Atlantic fisheries. The travels of Marco Polo and other Europeans through Asia were widely read, and voyages to the East began to appear a practical possibility. Under the influence of Prince Henry the Navigator, Portuguese seamen pushed farther and farther south down the fever-green coast of Africa. At last in 1487, half a lifetime after Henry's death, Bartholomew Diaz reached the southern tip, rounded the Cape of Good Hope, and found the Indian Ocean before him.

In 1497 Vasco da Gama with four ships reached India itself, purchased a cargo of spices and pepper, announced tersely that he had come "to seek Christians and Spices," and sailed back to his king with the news that the route to the sources of the Eastern trade lay open.

While the Portuguese had been edging ever southwards down the brawny African continent, Spanish eyes had been turned westwards.

Christopher Columbus sailed with his three ships, *Santa Maria*, *Nina*, and *Pinta*, in 1492, and believed he had reached the Indies when he touched on the outlying cays of the Bahamas. He christened his landfall San Salvador, to be renamed, by irreverent generations of later years, Rum Cay.

His new land, of course, was not the Indies. The immense bulk of North and South America lay in the way. But by accident he had touched on the fringes of the greatest gold and silver sources the world had known. The bullion wealth of Mexico alone was incredible, fantastic.

By 1522 Magellan's *Victoria* had sailed right around the globe, proving its roundness. In less than thirty short years the world — which for 2,000 years was believed to consist solely of Europe and Asia — was expanded to encompass the whole globe. Only Australia and the Arctic and Antarctic continents remained to be discovered. It was the greatest epoch of exploration in the history of the world. Nothing comparable had happened before. Nothing so significant has occurred since, up to the present day when we stand on the threshold of the exploration of Space.

The conquest of the new territories was accomplished astonishingly quickly and easily. Cortez and a ragged handful of veterans from the Moorish wars took Mexico with a few horses and cannon. The Conquistadors rode triumphantly into Bolivia and Peru, toppling the ancient Indian civilizations with contemptuous ease.

The Portuguese found, somewhat to their surprise, that the Turks and Arabs, who had been near-invincible with their fleet-footed cavalry on shore, were wholly vulnerable at sea in the Indian Ocean, The new European ships, bred from hard work on mid-Atlantic fishing grounds, sailed faster and manoeuvred more easily than the galleys which were the standard fighting units of the Mohammedan war fleets. These traditional Levantine vessels had banks of oars and huge single lateen sails, and were little changed from Roman galleys except for the addition of artillery. They were limited by their construction to one or two guns firing over the bow. The European ships had guns in banks and rows along their bulwarks, enabling them to fire broadsides. Outsailed and out-gunned, the galleys were defeated in a series of sea battles from the Red Sea to the Malacca Straits. European guns and sails were to dominate the East for centuries to come.

By the 1520s the Spaniards had discovered the Pacific and reached the Spice Islands by sailing westwards, and in 1529 the Catholic Spaniards and Portuguese, with Papal approval, divided the world between them by the Treaty of Saragossa. The New Worlds were discovered and conquered. The riches which all men desired were to hand.

And the crusade for Christ? Once the Moor was pushed back glowering behind his North African boundaries, the Turkish, Arab and Egyptian fleets in the Indian Ocean splintered and sunk by Portuguese cannonfire, and the trade

27

routes of Muslim severed, the old crusading zeals seemed less important. As the century wore on, the thoughts of the kings and conquistadors of Portugal and Spain turned more and more to the wealth, and how best to keep it a monopoly for ever and aye. They banned ships of other nations from sailing or trading in their colonial seas on pain of death. They built forts and manned garrisons, flogged and harried reluctant natives into the mines and plantations, and every year the heavily laden galleons rolled back across the oceans with the plunder.

The enemy, as time went by, became not so much the defeated anti-Christ Moor, but the wicked Protestant nations of England, France, and Holland, the emerging, aggressive, young countries, whose lusty pirates and freebooters were taking an increasing and unlawful interest in the wealth being won across the seas.

At first their expeditions were gadfly stings. But the Viking raids of Francis Drake and his compatriots on Spanish-American towns and shipping, covertly encouraged by Queen Elizabeth, kept Phillip of Spain in a cold fury. There grew in him a determination to crush the Heretics once and for all, and the instrument was to be the Great Armada of 1588. That Armada perished with blood-slippery decks in the iron hell of English cannonades, in the shrieking fury of the storms as the galleons fled around Scotland and Ireland, in a trail of shipwreck, and ruin, and floating corpses, all the way back to Cadiz . . . .

A disaster which led to the opening of the Indies to Dutch trade, the formation of the United East India Company in 1602, the Golden Age of Holland, and the voyage of the ship *Zeewyk* from Zeeland under skipper Jan Steyns in the year 1726.

4
Outward Bound

FOR SIX WET GREY DAYS, DECKS SOAKED AND SLIPPERY, THE *Zeewyk* rolled and pitched her way down the Channel. New hands lay and groaned helpless in their vomit below decks and slobbered in the scuppers when the bo'sun's mates whipped them topsides to stand watch.

The sea and spiteful wind found weaknesses in new gear, and experienced hands were kept aloft splicing with numbed fingers, re-making rigging, tightening slack stays and braces, and making an efficient working unit out of the new ship. Dressed in light calico clothing issued for the tropics, the men were continually shivering and cold in the bitter early winter weather.

Many of them were homesick and wept in their berths. The officers and petty officers were raw-tempered and snappish, and it was a miserable period for everyone. Even the toughest of the old hands was relieved when Steyns, with an oath flung to the contrary headwinds, had the helm put over and steered west towards England to drop anchor in the Roads of Downs; the sheltered waters at the mouth of the Thames Estuary where the shores of Kent sweep out in a bight towards France, and formed a friendly haven for sailing ships to drop their hooks and wait for favourable winds.

A nor-easter was the wind that the *Zeewyk* wanted. Blowing down the middle of the Channel to get them past the Goodwin Sands, Cape Griz Nez, Beachy Head, Alderney, The Lizard, and the Scilly Isles . . . all the sands, shoals, rocks and ship-traps of that stormy little sea, the English Channel. It has killed more ships and men than any other similar-sized stretch of water in the world, and still kills them today.

A nor'-easter they needed, but not a November ship-murdering gale screaming down ice-heavy out of the North. The Indiamen were built for ocean sailing runs, and not for manoeuvering blind in sleet or fog among restricted waters, or clawing off a lee shore.

Steel ships of today, with their humming turbines and watchful radar are only affected by the most exceptional weather. Arrivals are scheduled confidently weeks ahead, and the ships mostly keep them, gale or calm, but 200 years ago there was no such thing as a time-table in any but the broadest sense. Ships left during certain months in which they could hope for the winds they wanted, and from then on they were simply "expected." Fair winds or foul weather could make days or weeks of difference in their arrival time. Sometimes they never arrived at all.

While the crew scrubbed the dregs of sea-sickness out of the berths below and the colour came back to the cheeks of the landsmen, Steyns scanned his charts. The instructions were copious in detail and cautionary advice.

The Indiamen had been sailing the Atlantic and Indian Ocean routes for more than a century, and the wakes of the Dutchmen had criss-crossed those great oceans so often that there was hardly a mile of blue water over which they had not sailed. The logs of the skippers, all the information on wind and weather, were collated, and used as a basis for periodical revisions of the charts and sailing instructions.

Before sailing from Dutch ports, each skipper was issued

formally with the latest Mercator charts drawn up by the Company. The courses were marked in heavy lines, so that there could be no misunderstanding about the route to be taken.

Indiamen skippers were allowed a 300 mile-wide corridor in which to sail down the South Atlantic. Two lines bounded it on either side on the issued chart and they looked like wheel ruts on the parchment. The skippers laughed among themselves and called it the "Wagonweg," or "Waggon Track."

There were instructions for every leg of the voyage, and they sometimes seemed a little overdone. Caution was the keynote.

The VOC was a company with vociferous and demanding shareholders. Their concern for their investment was reflected in the proliferation of instructions which shepherded merchants and skippers through all their activities. Woe betide a Company servant if disaster occurred through disobeying them. Which makes all the more astounding the decision Jan Steyns reached, as a new skipper in his new ship, in May of the following year, off the Australian coast.

Beneath the yellow light of the lantern dappling the curved beams of the great stern cabin, Steyns must have read and re-read his instructions at the Roads of Downs. It would be interesting to know what thoughts passed through his mind; to discover whether the strange desire to visit the Australian coast, on which he was to risk his career, his ship, and his crew, had already taken root.

The *Zeewyk*, the newest and finest ship of the Zeeland fleet, was carrying a rich and varied cargo. Down in the holds were cases and kegs of liquor of many kinds; barrels of meat, pork, and fish; sacks of round, red Edam cheeses; heavy ironwork for Indies garrison gates; toys and trinkets for the Indies trade; powder and shot for her own thirty-eight guns; and an armoury of muskets and flintlock pistols. Indiamen were fighting ships, heavily armed against pirates.

In Steyns' own cabin were ten squat wooden treasure chests, which had been loaded at Vlissingen with an armed guard, and a lot of sweating solemnity. They weighed

600 pounds apiece, and it took several men to carry each one from the waggons. Signatures had been collected for security at every stage of the journey, starting at the Middelburg mint and with Steyns' flourish the last of all. There were brass bands and three locks on each chest.

In the chests were gold and silver bars, pieces-of-eight, rix dollars, ducatons, and small silver and copper coins, to a total value of 315,838 guilders. It was a consignment which seems fabulous even to modern eyes, but rich cargoes of precious metal were common on armed Indiamen. It was a time before cheque-books or letters of credit, and since precious metals and coins themselves increased in value in the East, they were a profitable export in their own right.

The value of the treasure was kept from the crew. For a man paid only ten guilders ($2.50) a month, the money in the chests represented an astronomical amount. No need to add to the normal temptations, and cut-throat inclinations of the common hands towards mutiny.

"For the sailors aboard Indiamen," wrote an eighteenth century traveller, "cursing, swearing, whoring, debauchery, and murder are mere trifles. There is always something brewing among these rascals and if their officers did not crack down on them quickly with punishments their own lives would not be safe for a moment among that unruly rabble."

There were procedures for keeping crews out of mischief. Prevention was better than cure, and it was preferable to have a man fall exhausted into his hammock at night, worn out, than to be continually whipping or worrying about him. The mates were ingenious at finding work for the hands. They painted and polished, scrubbed and holystoned already spotless decks. In fine weather they practised battle-stations and gunnery, or cleaned out below-decks with sprinklings of vinegar. They waved smoking sulphur torches in the reeking dark of the quarters, in a battle against lice and bugs, until they themselves were driven out by the choking fumes. The foul insects were seldom much incommoded.

The bo'sun kept the crew at their tasks. If they were slow they were smartened by a rope's end. Insolence fetched a tooth-loosening blow to the mouth from the bo'sun's knuckles, or a flogging if a more senior officer was involved.

Though the Directors of the Company decreed early in the days of sailing to the Indies that only "Good, trusty, Netherlands Hearts" should be employed on their vessels, the crews of Indiamen were often something of a League of Nations.

The *Zeewyk*'s muster roll, still preserved among VOC records, shows that forty-one percent of her crew were foreigners—eighty-six of the 208 men who went aboard her for the start of the autumn outward voyage—and they represented thirteen nationalities, including one Russian, Maarten Dirksz, a gunner from St Petersburg.

There were Germans, Danes, Belgians, Frenchmen, Swiss, Britishers, Swedes, Norwegians, Italian, Portuguese. The spelling of their names on the Company roll was in phonetic Dutch, set down the way the unfamiliar syllables fell on the ear of the VOC clerk of the moment. So that George Forkson, the Scottish third officer from Edinburgh, became "Joris Forkson" on the roll. Another Briton, Jonathan Wright from London, was written down as "Johannes Riet." We may imagine how mangled some of the tongue-tripping French, Polish and Swiss names became in the transfer from their owners' lips to the Company's parchment.

Germans and Belgians—twenty-seven of each—made up the bulk of the foreign complement of the *Zeewyk*. While only two of the officers and petty officers (third mate Forkson and the French petty officer in charge of rigging, David Gossier from Dieppe) were non-Dutch, some twenty of the forty-five seamen aboard were foreign; twenty-one out of the thirty-one gunners; and thirty-three of the seventy-three soldiers were from nations other than the seven provinces of the Netherlands.

The stolid Belgians, predictably, were mostly enlisted as soldiers. Perhaps surprisingly, because Germany is usually thought of as a military nation, nearly half the Germans were seamen.

Dutch views on foreigners in the Indies fleet varied. Nicolas Witsen, the scholar, remarked in 1671 (*The Dutch*

East Indiamen, Their sailors, their navigators, and Life on Board, 1602-1795; Professor C. R. Boxer) that a mixture of nationalities lessened the chances of mutiny. But others claimed that foreigners, and in particular the English and French, were trouble-makers and recalcitrants.

But the Company had little choice. Crews in the 1600s were almost exclusively Netherlanders, but by 1727—due to the heavy death rate, a shortage of experienced men, and perhaps the reputation of Indies voyages—the recruiting officers for ships like the *Zeewyk* had to sign on a complement which was half foreigners, in order to fill their muster rolls.

Later in the century the situation became even worse. European seamen of any nationality became so scarce that the Dutch, who recoiled from using the infamous press-gang by which the English kidnapped unwilling men into service, signed on Asiatics—Chinese, Malays, Indians from the coast of Gujarat, and even Japanese. All these were excellent seamen in their own latitudes, but tended to succumb to cold on the European voyages and died easily.

Oddly, Negroes did not seem to mind the cold as much as Asiatics, and were frequently found on English and French ships, though rarely on Dutch East Indiamen. However, the *Zeewyk* did sign on two West Indians: Anthony Kerspes and Joost Bruggeman. Neither survived the voyage.

Watches fell to all hands, regardless of country, creed or colour and were four hours on duty, eight hours off, except in difficult waters like the Channel or in heavy weather when three four-hour watches were stood in every twenty-four hours.

There were so many sea deaths aboard Indiamen that while three watches were rostered on outward-bound vessels like the *Zeewyk*, many short-handed homeward-bounders had to reduce to two. Indiamen carried big crews of up to 200 men, whereas the famous clippers of the nineteenth century, vessels like the *Cutty Sark* and *Thermopylae* which had more sails and more work, usually had less than thirty hands. The extra seamen on East Indiamen were carried as replacements and because of the appalling loss of life aboard ships voyaging to the tropics.

34

The biggest shipboard killer was scurvy, caused by a deficiency of vitamin C. It was vaguely understood that fresh greens, fruit, and rainwater were a remedy, but that was like saying the best cure for seasickness was to sit under a shady tree. The journey to the Indies took so long that it was impossible to keep fresh provisions for the full distance. Some ships carried live pigs, chickens, and goats, and some even grew vegetables in tubs. But inevitably, in the stinking dripping atmosphere below decks, fresh food soon went bad. The scurvy symptoms of spots, swollen limbs, and loose and bleeding teeth would begin to show among the crew after a few weeks at sea.

The deaths were usually proportionate to the length of the voyage. On a quick passage, a ship might get through with no deaths at all. Others, which were many months *en route* had appalling tolls.

The Zeeland ship *Zuytdorp* sailed from the *Zeewyk's* home port of Vlissengen, or Flushing, in 1711, together with a smaller consort ship, the *Belvliet*. They took an unusually long time — seven months instead of the normal three to four — to reach the Cape of Good Hope, and the *Zuytdorp* lost 112 men out of a crew of 286 during this first leg of the voyage. Twenty-two sick men, some near death, were carried ashore to hospital in Cape Town. The *Belvliet* had sixty deaths, including her skipper Dirk Blauw and the commander of the soldiers, out of a complement of 164. When the *Belvliet* finally reached Batavia, only four of the fifty-eight soldiers who had marched aboard in their fine uniforms were still alive. The *Zuytdorp* was wrecked, and the men who had survived the sickness perished miserably on barren Australian shores.

Sailing times to the Indies varied considerably. In 1639 two ships, the *Haarlem* and *Nieuw Amsterdam*, flew to the Sunda Straits in 115 and 114 days without stopping at the Cape — a fantastic four months for the entire journey. They arrived with all men fit and well.

This legendary performance was often talked about in later years, but never again equalled. In the 1700s, the time for the voyage was more frequently from seven to nine months, including a welcome stop-over of ten to twenty days at the Cape where sick men were landed and fresh crew and provisions taken on.

Death rates fluctuated from ship to ship. There were some terrible voyages, such as that of the fleet of ten ships which left Holland in 1782 with 2,653 men aboard and arrived at the Cape after losing 1,095 *en route*; a death-rate of 43 per cent. Of the survivors, 915 were so sick that they had to be carried ashore to hospital. And this at the half-way mark of the outward voyage!

The average death-rate for a single three-year tour of duty in the East Indies was from a quarter to one-third of the men who enlisted, depending to an extent on where they were sent. Some plague spots took terrible toll, while other posts were comparatively healthy. A man who survived one tour seemed to gain an immunity to many of the tropic diseases, and his chances were better thereafter. Old hands were valued on this account. The unhealthy site of the capital of Batavia, centre of all the VOC Indies activities, and the first and last port of call, contributed greatly to the death-rate.

Mortalities increased so dramatically in Batavia after the digging of a new canal in 1731 that anyone who could do so moved to houses out of town. Even the Governor refused to reside in the historic Fort on the seafront, the traditional seat of government, after 1741. Surgeon Hamilton of H.M.S. *Pandora* described Batavia in 1791 as a "Golgotha . . . a painted sepulchre, which buries its whole settlement every five years."

When Captain James Cook, the great English Pacific navigator, arrived at Batavia in H.M.S. *Endeavour* in 1770, after discovering Australia's east coast, he wrote in his journal with justifiable pride that after two years at sea "Not one man has been lost by sickness during the whole voyage." He made his boast too soon, because after a short time at Batavia most of the crew of the *Endeavour* were stricken with dysentery or malaria, and seven died. Cook himself, with Joseph Banks and the Swedish naturalist Solander, became critically ill.

"The curve of the battered shape was familiar, if unexpected . . . the tusk was the sure sign of an old shipwreck close at hand."

The *Endeavour* fled from the equator fever port. But the sickness, "fever and the bloody flux," had signed aboard, and she dropped her canvas-sewn dead with a cannon shot at their feet all the way across the Indian Ocean, making a death's-head jest of Cook's log entry.

Death was to become a familiar visitor to the *Zeewyk* men. It claimed thirty of them on the run down the South Atlantic, and many more in its own good time at a place of strange reefs and low white islands.

If they had known what lay before them, they might have been less eager to sign on in Holland. But there was no reason to suppose that the voyage would be anything out of the ordinary. In fact many of the men sitting down to mess as the *Zeewyk* swung at anchor in the Downs probably congratulated themselves on having joined a well-found ship with good victuals.

They had salt beef twice a week, on Sundays and Tuesdays, and smoked pork on Thursdays. On other days they had "stockfish"; dried and salted cod and herring. The vegetables were mainly barley and dried beans or peas, with prunes and rice as a cook's speciality on Sundays. The men ate in messes of up to ten men apiece, taking it in turns to act as orderly to bring the food from the galley, and perfunctorily wash down the wooden spoons and bowls, and the eating board.

The officers sat at the skipper's table in order of seniority. Jan Steyns had the table head, then there was the merchant Jan Nebbens, first mate Pieter Langeweg, second mate Adriaen van der Graeff, Jan d'Bood the chief surgeon, Pieter Vleke the commander of the soldiers, Leendert Vloo the preacher or predikant, and Joris Forkson the third mate. They had a proper table with a cloth, napkins, pewter plates and spoons, and a choice of food and liquor.

These men were the Ship's Council. Dutch ships were more democratic than those of most nations, and difficult or out-of-the-ordinary decisions were arrived at by the Council together with the skipper.

Homosexuality was a serious problem among men confined in close quarters for months without women. The

This model of the Dutch East Indiaman *Padmos* is of a ship which would have been very much the same as the *Zeewyk*

Dutch called it "the stupid sin" and it was regarded severely, sometimes being punished by death. This sin, and the subsequent executions, were to throw dark shadows over the lives of the *Zeewyk* men at a later time, when the world believed them dead and they had been without women for a long time.

Included in the food were generous dosages of saltpetre, which was supposed to "cool the flesh" and reduce the men's urge towards unnatural acts.

The quality and quantity of food aboard depended on the cook. Dishonest seacooks cheated on rations and pocketed the money issued to buy provisions, but they risked a severe beating with their cooking utensils if the crew found them out.

The cook of the *Zeewyk* was listed on the ship's muster roll as Everd Bloncke Byle; a French name spelled by a Dutch clerk. There is no comment on his cooking, but he was to survive all the adventures.

At four o'clock every morning all hands were issued with a glass of brandy. This must have hit their empty stomachs hard at that chill hour, but it was intended to put them in good heart for the coming day. The Dutch believed devoutly that strong drink strengthened the stomach, and helped to prevent fever and the flux. There was always a whiff of liquor on the whiskers of an Indiaman's crew.

The *Zeewyk* men received the usual variety of grog. Beer was served every day as long as it lasted, and since it went bad in the tropics they drank it quickly. As well as the morning brandy, rations of French and Spanish wine were ladled out daily, with extra brandy on special occasions. Alcohol was deemed to be specially beneficial on an empty stomach. Boatswains, cooks, and carpenters received a double ration, and boys a half. It had to be swallowed on the spot, because hoarding was prohibited for fear of drunken brawls. Alcohol, the stronger the better, was the standard preventative medicine for all diseases. And if you died — well, at least you died drunk.

Sick parades were summonsed twice a day, by the provost, or master-at-arms, banging his baton on the mainmast and bawling out an official call in his stentorian voice.

Chief surgeon Jan d'Bood was assisted by the second and third surgeons, Melgioor d'Johghe and Jan Vroom. The chief had officer status, and the second and third surgeons were ranked as petty officers, but—perhaps because of their doubtful results—surgeons were not particularly highly regarded aboard Indiamen.

They got their jobs after satisfying a panel of physicians on the subjects of blood-letting and cauterizing wounds, and showing that they could set bones, treat musket wounds, burns, bruises, gangrene, and the suppurating sores of the seaman's curse, scurvy. They had to be able to stitch up a gash, close off a vein, or saw off an arm or leg—the last without anaesthetic, the man's mates plying him with brandy and holding him down—and cauterizing the stump with boiling tar to stop the bleeding. There was little enough for the surgeons to do in the early stages of the voyage, for only time could cure sea-sickness. But there would be work for them later.

The *Zeewyk* waited ten days in the Downs for a favourable wind. Jan Steyns paced his quarter deck; head back and eyes searching the grey sky for the new clouds that would mean a wind change. Worrying that every day of delay took them closer to mid-winter, and the chance of being over-whelmed at the anchorage by a seasonal gale of exceptional ferocity.

Everyone was relieved when, on 23 November 1726, the wind at last swung to the north, and the bo'sun bawled the crew to the capstans. They lost two anchors and one and a half cables before they could clear the Downs, and the skipper was red faced and furious. But at least she was away down Channel.

5
Scurvy and Smuggling

On a day of dust and heat on the south african veldt in the year 1725, while the *Zeewyk* was still a skeleton of ribs and frames in the shipbuilders' yard, some African hunters killed an elephant.

It was a cruel business. The hunters were so poorly armed, with their short iron-tipped spears and frail knives compared with the huge strength and armoured hide of their adversary, that they had to defeat him a little at a time.

First they had crippled him with a trap—a sprung sapling which had staked his leg and prevented the terrible charge which was more than any of the hunters could withstand. Then they had pursued him, bleeding, until he became exhausted. When he turned at bay they flung their cloaks or karosses over his head to blind and distract him and one of the hunters, braver than the rest, slipped a spear into his belly through his loins at the rear. Death was a long time coming. The elephant trumpeted in rage and pain, the flies swarmed as the blood flowed, and the hunters waited round him in a circle for the end.

It was primaeval as a pack of wolves pulling down a stag. A hunting ritual little changed since Stone Age days. But the reasons had altered. The Bantu natives killed the elephant not for his flesh but for the curving ivory tusks. The tusks had no value to them—unlike the hairy mane of a lion which warriors wore proudly as a sign of courage—but they could be bartered at a frontier post for iron axes, knives, coloured blankets, mirrors, and gew-gaws.

The gruff Dutch farmers and the devious Arab traders who made periodic journeys through the country beyond the Graaff-Reinet frontier land which would later be fought over by the fierce Zulus and Matabele tribes were eager for ivory, and it fetched high prices in illegal sale at the Cape.

African ivory was the best in the world, being far superior in size and grain to the smaller tusks of Asian elephants. There was a universal market for it, with buyers in London, Amsterdam, Cairo, Damascus, India, China, Japan, and Indonesia. It was used for ornamental carving for everything from cardinal's buttons to crucifixes, chess-sets to candle-sticks, sword-hilts to billiard balls.

It was a bloody trade because the poor elephants had to be killed to part them from their tusks, and for the killing the muskets of 1726 and for many years afterwards were not reliable or powerful enough to stop a charging bull. So the slaughter was mainly performed by groups of native hunters with means so primitive that they were often killed themselves. But life was cheap in Africa. You could buy a sulky African captive in his home grass hut country for a few guilders, though the slave traders charged a pretty price once they had shipped him to a market in fetters.

The slave trade and the ivory trade went hand in hand. Twin trades of misery. The first task of a slave newly-bought in the interior—12 million were taken from West Africa alone over 300 years—was usually to carry ivory to the coast. The tusks weighed as much as 200 pounds each in very exceptional animals, but averaged eighty to ninety pounds.

Though the VOC officially bought in several tons of tusks through its East African trading post at Delagoa Bay, opened in 1721 but closed in 1730 because fever killed off too many white men, most elephant tusks came into the Cape Colony illegally, and were smuggled out to ships as contraband.

The Cape, like Batavia, was a Vereenigde Oost-Indische Compagnie town, and free trade with the outside world was strictly forbidden. Every item, however small and unimportant, was supposed to be bought and sold through the VOC monopoly, and Cape Town was regarded officially as being only a victualling post for East Indiamen on their way to and from the Indies.

But English and French ships called there also, and the poorly-paid Company servants at the Cape were eager to supplement their incomes, so it became a smuggler's paradise. Pearls, gems, necklaces, carved ivory, silks, tea, spices, porcelain—any items easily concealed in a sea-chest or among the ballast below—were brought from the East and smuggled ashore at the Cape, where they were sold to visiting ships in clandestine negotiation. Company servants going out to the East usually smuggled money, because the big silver Rix Dollar, worth 66 stuivers at home, fetched 78 stuivers in the exchange markets of the East. So many were carried out of Holland that a shortage was created in the homeland, and the VOC vainly passed laws forbidding their export.

Prohibitions, pleas, edicts, threats, were in vain. All the Company's servants gleefully dealt in contraband whenever they were able, and their trade activities on the side sometimes exceeded the business they did for the Company.

It was said that the post of senior merchant in Japan was worth 30,000 guilders a year in illegal income, and men were willing to pay huge bribes for lucrative positions. Governor General van Hoorn had come smiling home from Batavia in 1709 with a fortune estimated at 10 million guilders, many hundred times his salary.

The VOC was well aware of what was going on—the smuggling was so great it sometimes affected market prices in Europe to the detriment of legal cargoes—but they were powerless to prevent it because the very inspectors and fiscal advocates who were supposed to police the regulations were also up to their necks in bribes and illegal trade.

Occasionally there were savage punishments. The whole town of Batavia turned pale when Governor Zwaardecroon hanged twenty men on a single day in 1722.

But it had so little lasting effect that most of the senior officers of the *Zeewyk*, and any of the crew who had the money, were carrying smuggled coin as she sailed towards the equator in January of 1727. The most deeply involved of all were her skipper, Jan Steyns, and the next most senior person aboard, the merchant Jan Nebbens.

The causes of the illegal trade were a combination of the temptations of distant posts in the East where Company servants often had little surveillance from the central base at Batavia, combined with miserly wages. The VOC, like many another great company in history, was so greedy for its profits that it resented paying its servants anything at all, and wages were universally low even for the standards of the day. So their servants cheated them, and despite floggings, hangings, and similar examples made of the occasional wretches unlucky enough to be caught, they mostly got away with it. The Company lamented the situation in edicts such as that posted at the Cape in 1719: "The lawlessness of the sailors instead of diminishing through fear of punishment seems on the contrary to obstinately increase."

In the year 1728 those of the *Zeewyk* men who were still alive were to be the subject of some unusual judgments on smuggling in the High Courts of Batavia. But that lay in the future. Possibly the only thoughts which Jan Steyns and Jan Nebbens had about the matter, as the *Zeewyk* dipped southwards towards the tropics, were whether they would be able to get hold of some ivory at the Cape at the right price. The tusks were waiting, including those of the young bull which the Bantus had killed. So was a coral reef many thousands of miles away.

The fated *Zeewyk* made a fine sight as she swung down past the Azores and Cape Verde Islands, shaping her course along the Wagon Track and laying over towards the shores of South America under the steady Trade Winds.

The first Portuguese ships sailing to the Indies had hugged the African coast. Calms under the land made a long voyage of it. Anopheles mosquitoes rose in black clouds from the swamps and river mouths each sunset, and men died in delirium from their malarial bites. They did not connect the mosquitoes with the deaths, merely regarding them as a nuisance, but blamed poisonous vapours from the jungle. *Malaria* actually means "bad air." Skippers found it healthier and quicker to sail the open sea, and at least they were right in keeping away from the estuarine marshes. In the open ocean were winds blowing so reliably towards the Americas that the early navigators gratefully called them the Trade Winds.

The Dutch found that by following these almost to the coast of South America, then riding the Brazil current south, they picked up a zone of boisterous westerlies in the South Atlantic below the present latitude of Rio. These blew them across to the Cape of Good Hope with taut sails and singing rigging, and they made passages in much shorter time than on a direct route. So they sailed a zig-zag dog-leg course down the Atlantic, and in the Indian Ocean they travelled in a great swinging half-circle for similar reasons.

In both the central tropic areas of the Atlantic and Indian Ocean there were areas of glassy calm known as the Doldrums. Ships could drift on the brassy sea, sails limp and the heat opening cracks in the deck, for days and weeks while men died daily from sickness, food rotted, and water turned green and slimy. They avoided the calms in the Atlantic by the Trade Wind route.

In the Indian Ocean a skipper called Henrik Brouwer, later to become a famous admiral and a governor at Batavia, was blown south of the Cape in 1611 and in latitudes above forty degrees south picked up the full-blooded westerly winds called the Roaring Forties by clipper captains of a later generation. He scudded before them across the Indian Ocean faster than anyone had ever travelled before and 3,000 miles out from the Cape ran into convenient southerlies which blew him up to the Sunda Straits, skirting the Doldrums altogether. He was delighted with his discovery and soon all the Indiamen skippers were following Brouwer's route.

The *Zeewyk*, sailing the same seas 115 years later, was not vastly different from Brouwer's ship to a landsman's eye. But a seaman would notice the changes which had taken place. Though the Dutch still retained the mediaeval poop and forecastle—and were laughed at as old-fashioned by the English and French—the features were less exaggerated than in Brouwer's day. Much less of a Fairy Castle, though she did look rather like a fat, dignified duck from certain angles.

A good deal of the gilt and gingerbread ornamentation, beloved of the 1600s, had gone too, though there were still carved figures around her stern window, and a flourish of filigree on the galleries, which were simply richly decorated privies for the officers. The common hands and crew performed their natural functions through and from the grill-work around the bow-sprit in front of the fore-peak at the head of the ship—hence the traditional Navy term for "Going to the Head." Often the sailors got wet and doused in foul weather, and feared to go for'ard in a gale, especially at night. There were strict regulations against men defecating or relieving themselves below. Nevertheless they often did so, and though the Dutch ships were considered exceptionally clean, the Portuguese and French ships were notorious stenchpits with bilges foul as sewers.

The men, of course, did not understand the connection between personal dirt and disease. They blamed fever on foul vapours and exhalations; dysentery and gastric complaints on anything except their own filthy habits.

Even on the cleanest vessels in the 1700s, the standard of hygiene was a long way below that expected of a sailor today. Men seldom changed their clothes unless they got wet. They hardly ever washed, and then only in lick-and-a-promise fashion, believing that soap and water dangerously dried out the natural oils of the body. Toilet paper as an invention for the comfort and convenience of mankind lay a long way in the future.

Lice and bed-bugs, *Cimex lectularius*, were accepted with

resignation as part of life both afloat and ashore, but you had less chance of escape aboard ship. Everyone scratched and itched, at a time when it was as accepted that people had lice as inevitably as dogs had fleas. It was possible to get rid of them, but since everyone else had them you became re-infected and so it was hardly worth the trouble. They lived in the crannies and woodwork of the ships with three-inch cockroaches which were known to eat away the finger- and toenails of sleeping men with gentle rasping, and a variety of other insects, including legions of hopping fleas and other less salubrious insects such as crab lice and sometimes the rat fleas, carriers of typhus which killed both its rodent hosts and men. Seamen did not complain over-much about the pests, because in those days no one knew what it was like to be without them.

The *Zeewyk* was listed as a ship of 145 feet in the East India Company register. She was a *Retour Schipp*, or return-vessel, one of the large armed merchantmen designed specifically for the task of cramming as much cargo in her holds as could be conveniently carried between the East and the Netherlands. Coastal trading at home and in the Indies employed smaller craft—flutes, galiots, yachts, and hookers. The size of the VOC ocean ships such as the *Zeewyk* was limited by the shallow waters of the approaches to Netherlands ports. Because the VOC standardized its vessels for convenience of calculating cargo capacity, providing spare parts for damaged vessels and so on, the return-vessels were built in lengths of 130, 145, or 160 feet.

The measurement was taken from the inside of the stem post at the bow to the inside of the rudder post. By the time the stern overhang—the Dutch ships were called "hag-boats" because of their transom sterns—the beak and bowsprit were considered, she was probably over 200 feet in length. She was 40 feet in the beam width amidships, 40 feet from keel to poop deck, and she drew three fathoms, or 18 feet of water under sail.

She was quite a large vessel, even by modern standards, and with all sails set would have taken up as much space on the skyline as a 10-storey block of flats. She lumbered along at a painfully slow three or four knots because of her wallowing, cargo-carrying design, and took two to three miles to complete a reverse change of course.

We tend today to think of the old sailing ships as being tiny, and indeed Columbus' *Santa Maria*, and the Portuguese caravels and carracks, were small craft with hulls hardly bigger than modern harbour ferries. Cook's *Endeavour* was only eighty feet long, Bligh's *Bounty* not much bigger, and Drake did much of his pirating in vessels scarcely bigger than a lugger. These were all famous craft and their size is often quoted. But there was a reason for this. The smaller craft were the most suitable for exploration and pirating because they manoeuvred easily in unknown seas. They could be careened to have the weed and barnacles scraped from their bottoms and leaks stopped in bays at the end of the world; an important factor in four-year voyages. They dodged easily and lightly among reefs and shallows. They were the jeeps of their day, able to go off the roads and beaten tracks and make their own paths.

The large merchant ships, and particularly the huge Indiamen, were like modern semi-trailer trucks, or road freight trains, designed for carrying maximum cargo in a straight line, but in peril as soon as they deviated from the highway. The Spanish built some huge galleons for their Pacific run from Manila to Acapulco, such as the 2,000-ton *Santissima Trinidad* captured by the British off San Bernadino Straits in 1762. In contrast the *Cutty Sark* built in 1876 was only 963 tons, and most of the crack clippers were under 1,000 tons.

The 145 feet VOC ships like the *Zeewyk* were the preferred class for the Company in 1726 because they could negotiate the shallow home port entrances and carry a fat cargo in their capacious holds, and still be handled easily. They normally carried about 150 seamen and 50 soldiers for Indies garrisons, but because of deaths were much more lightly crewed on the homeward run.

The English thought the Dutch Indiamen were very old fashioned because of their high poops and forecastles and their sailing rig.

In the early 1600s the Dutch had been in the forefront of ship design and building, and sold merchant ships to all other seafaring nations in Europe, including England and Sweden. The 1628 *Vasa*, whose hull was recently raised from Stockholm harbour, was built by a Netherlands master shipwright, Henrik Hybertsson, to a Dutch design for King Gustaf Adolf of Sweden. The efficient Dutch soon discovered the advantages of uniform designs for the ordering of timber lengths, prefabricating sections of ships, and getting a scale of known costs from the shipwrights, but standardization also had an inherent danger. It halted the evolution of new designs, and Dutch shipwrights became staid traditionalists, resisting any changes or innovations. Their designs became fixed and static while other nations constantly improved their vessels, running gear, and sail rigs.

So it was that in 1726 the *Zeewyk* had a deep waist and high poop and forecastle like ships of a previous century, while many English and French ships of her time had modern frigate or flush decking from bow to stern. The frigate decks shed gale seas coming over the rail like water from a duck's back. Waist decks tended to accumulate tons of green water in dangerous top-weight before it drained, increasing the risk of broaching or capsizing, or of flooding below.

More important, in view of what was to happen to her, *Zeewyk* also had a square steering sail stuck up on a little mast on the end of her bowsprit, called a "blind sail" because it obscured vision ahead. This had been superseded on English and French merchantmen by the triangular jibs and head-sails still commonly used today, and which allow much quicker manoeuvring and changing of courses. Dutch fishing boats and small craft had also switched to jibs by the 1700s, but the East India Company clung doggedly to old ways.

If the *Zeewyk* had been fitted with jibs they might have been able to save her.

She crossed the Tropic of Cancer on 21 December 1726, leaving behind the winter snows softly falling to blanket Europe in a white shroud. By New Year's Day of 1727 the ship was close to the equator. Skies were blue and flying fish burst in shoals from under her forefoot to skim on outstretched wings across the glinting surface of the sea. The sun shone brightly, and after the weeks of bitter weather early in the voyage the *Zeewyk* men had hatches and gun-ports open to dry the mildew and stink out of the dark dank quarters below.

The men sang as they worked, and the second mate Adriaen van der Graeff penned his daily entries in his journal in a spirit of cheerful optimism. These were sun-smiling days in flying fish latitudes with warm starry nights and songs on deck in the evenings.

They had been practising battle drill. Drumming the hands to action stations at the battle call *"Overal! . . . Overal!"* Opening the red-painted gun ports and running the black, ugly guns out to fire on command at floating casks and boxes tossed overside as targets, until they knew the routine backwards.

Then, after the make-believe and shadow-sparring there was a real enemy on 3 January 1727.

The trumpets blew noisily. Drums beat and sent the blood pulsing. Van der Graeff wrote in his journal: "Before noon, at about 10 o'clock the soldier Jan Loser of Hamburg dies. Shortly after the other ship fired a gun and shortened sail, and turned to leeward against us, and ran up a flag which we could not recognize. We ran up the standard of the Republic and drew up our men in line of battle. . . ."

"Overal! . . . Overal!" Bare feet beat a tattoo on decks and ladders, men bumping into each other with breathless curses in the darkness below decks.

All hammocks and bedding were lashed up in nets to absorb lethal flying splinters of woodwork when enemy balls crashed into their ship. The guns were unchocked and their heavy fixed lashings replaced by springy block-and-tackles as snubbers against recoil. Powder and shot were hauled on deck in baskets, and the cannonballs placed in boxes or hoops to stop them rolling about the deck. Bar shot, and chain shot, and grape shot for the little bronze breech-loading guns on the upper decks were run up in the lifts.

The gunners stood by with their long spiral slow matches, their gun crews ready with reamers to scrape out hot sparks from the barrel and swabbers to quench the guns' heat and prevent a premature explosion. The junior powder monkeys, flushed and eager, ran with the brass and canvas measures of powder. Sand was sprinkled underfoot to stop the gunners slipping on blood-greasy decks. Muskets, bandoleers, cutlasses, and pikes, were handed out by the provost's mates, and seamen scrambled aloft with chains to reinforce the rigging in case it should be cut through by bar shot. A detail of the soldiers, clumsy and unsure of their footing, were sent up to the cross-trees with their muskets to act as marksmen from above.

The means of killing and maiming were prepared. Down below the surgeon and his mates made ready for the *Zeewyk*'s bloody part of the bargain; the treatment of the wounded and dying. The saw-bones stood behind their table of polished and glinting instruments. Neatly laid out were saws, knives, mallets, needles, gut, ligatures, bowls, and bandages. Now all was ready.

The mates took their stations purposefully by the ladders, each with a loaded pistol ready to shoot men deserting their posts under fire.

The bo'sun with his picked squad of sail-handlers waited the skipper's command . . . all eyes peered at the black sea-distant silhouette of the stranger. Soldiers looked down uncertainly from aloft in the fighting-tops. Gunners squinted through the squares of gun-ports painted bright red so that blood spilt on the gun decks would not show so raw. Officers watched the foreign ship through the maddeningly indistinct blur of a telescope, all hands praying for her to close as the strange sail paced them on the horizon. Was she Spaniard, English privateer, or French Indiaman? Warship, pirate, or trader?

They never found out. For forty-eight hours of suspense they remained chafing at readiness. But after the second day she sheered away and they had the anti-climax of putting away their arms without a shot having been fired. They were disappointed.

50

It may seem strange for men to wish for the sulphurous hell of a battle at sea. Scuppers red with blood. Shrieks of the wounded and dying. . . . The concussive thump of cannon. . . .

But there was the prize money. Everyone shared in a capture.

The crew's division amounted to one sixteenth of the prize to be split in proportion to their wages, and with a rich capture this could be a considerable sum by their standards. It was the one chance of an Indiaman's crew to add legitimately to their wages, and they were always eager for a sea-fight. Besides it was a chance for glory and a break from the dullness of brute stupid work. Every man secretly fancied himself a hero, and having worked themselves up into a truculent frame of mind, the *Zeewyk* men put their cutlasses away and closed their gunports with disappointment and mutterings about cowardly scum in foreign vessels.

They had already been boarded unobtrusively by the advance party of a deadlier enemy. Scurvy.

They had now been many weeks at sea. The symptoms of spots, loosening teeth and lethargy, all too familiar to experienced seamen, began to show themselves. All the beer was gone and the fresh food with it. The tepid water in the barrels had grown a green scum and stank so much that they held their noses when they drank it. But their thirst had increased because the main diet was now salt and smoked provisions, and dry biscuits. Weevils rioted in the biscuits and the larvae squirmed among the dried beans, peas, and prunes. The butter was rancid oil in the heat. The sun, "that brass bastard," as the Dutch called him in the tropics, beat down more and more heavily. Scurvy's favourite boarding ground was the tropics.

The scourge took different courses with different men, but usually the first warning was continual tiredness; a general hard-to-define feeling of listlessness and lassitude. When teeth began to loosen in their gums, the mouth bled, and the breath became foul the disease had a serious hold. Limbs developed livid spots, and joints swelled until the spots burst open and became suppurating, non-healing sores. The scurvy was accompanied by generalized aches and pains, and a pathological anxiety.

Men wept at trivial things. Sometimes old wounds opened up. A man confined to his hammock would get up, feeling better, and drop dead from the slightest exertion. The longer the voyage the more deaths, the longer the sick-list.

The parade before the mainmast for treatment grew longer daily, and so did the list of men who were unable to climb the ladders and lay helpless below. They began burying them one after the other, sewn up in canvas by the sailmaker with a cannonball at their feet, and launched over the bulwarks with a short prayer and a splash . . . a notation in the daily register for the pay clerk in Holland to close their account.

Under the stern, in permanent station behind the wake were the fins of the ship-followers, sharks. They ate the scraps from the galley, the ship's offal, and probably the scurvy victims, snapped up before the cannon shot could decently carry them down into the deeps. At least the seamen believed so and shook their fists at them and occasionally when becalmed they fished for them, dragging the huge thrashing snapping bodies up on deck to chop them in pieces with knives and hatchets. All sailing ship men loathed and hated sharks—they knew what would happen if they fell overboard.

On 10 February there was another call to action stations. Again the trumpets sounded and the drums and bare feet beat their tattoo. But this ship, too, sheered away from the heavy armament of the *Zeewyk*. So far, eleven seamen, one soldier, and the gunner had died. Christiaen Melo was promoted up into his place in charge of the gun deck.

The *Zeewyk* crossed the Tropic of Capricorn on 18 February. Day followed day. The sick line got longer, the food worse, and the songs and jokes faded from the scurvy-chapped lips of the crew. Most of them had mild symptoms of scurvy. Every man had a dark fear in his stomach as he watched the burials. There was a stink of death down below, and many preferred to sleep on deck.

Details of the *Padmos* model, showing the characteristic design of a Dutch East Indiaman. Officers and passengers would have lived in the accommodation under the poop (top photograph). The windows of the "great cabin" can be seen in the stern

At last on 25 March 1727, they raised the sugar lump silhouette of Table Mountain, and a cheer went up from the hands on deck. It was feebly echoed by the lips of the despairing sick below who now renewed hope of life. If they could only get ashore in time. . . .

Thirty-six were bed-ridden, and certified as too ill to continue the voyage. Allowing for the fact that all the crew would get three weeks recuperation at the Cape, this meant they were closer to death than life. Thirty men had died at sea in the five months since leaving Holland.

The anchors splashed down in the roadstead in Table Bay on 26 March, among eighteen other vessels of the Company. Three were jubilantly homeward bound, the rest, like the *Zeewyk*, on their way out to the Indies. Even before the anchors had dropped, the *Zeewyk* crew were shaving and trimming hair and beards, and preening themselves for a run ashore. Cape Town was notoriously hospitable, and lived up to its name as The Tavern of the Seas.

It was founded in 1652 as a half-way house to provide fresh food and a hospital for Indies shipping. Officially it only existed to serve Company purposes, but the burghers were a remarkably obstinate lot and seemed to have missed the point. They had shown a great deal more initiative in farming, wine-growing, and cattle-raising than the Company intended or approved. In fact the Cape, despite all attempts to limit it to the status of shore station by the Directors, had become a colony by 1727. It was to expand more and more as the century progressed.

After five months at sea the *Zeewyk* men were not interested in the colonial condition or problems of the Cape. They made straight for the taverns to work off their accumulated thirsts and continence. The Last Penny, The Red Ox, The Blue Anchor were glad to assist them and take their money. Drunken seamen and soldiers with crews of other ships lined up outside the Company's Slave Lodge to bid for strong-limbed Negro, Malay, and mulatto girls for a night, boasting sailor-fashion of the strength of their desire and capabilities, while the girls smiled. They knew that after the drink and the

TOP: The bluff bows of a vessel of the *Zeewyk* class. The design of the Dutch East Indiamen changed very little over more than a century. BOTTOM: Amidships section of an East Indiaman

months at sea the men would be quickly exhausted, and with any luck they would be able to sell themselves "for the night" several times in one evening.

The sick were transported to the hospital. With graveyard humour it was sometimes called "The Cemetery," because of the deaths which occurred there. Nonetheless the clean air, the fruit and fresh meat of the Cape gave the thirty-six *Zeewyk* men more hope than they had at sea. And if they recovered they would certainly stand a better chance aboard another vessel than the men who were to sail in the *Zeewyk* on her last sea miles.

The invalids were replaced by twelve new men, hands who had been left sick by earlier ships and were considered fit now to go on with their duty. They signed aboard on 5 April, and joined the crew in unloading cargo which seems to have been mainly flat grey bricks for Cape streets and buildings— 4,038 pounds of them. A donkey, intended for the Cape, had died at sea.

While the men were swilling in the taverns and rutting with any woman, black or white, who would have them, the officers moved in rather more elevated social circles among the burghers and their families. But their instincts were the same. The officers were human, too, and their eyes flickered hungrily over the faces of the ladies, searching for an answering glance. . . .

On one of the pleasant evenings with wine and slave music—for the burghers of the Cape were very hospitable— probably the first probing suggestions were put out about the tusks.

The negotiations would have been conducted with delicacy and discretion. After all there were penalties if they were caught. The price was agreed after some haggling and the tusks were smuggled aboard at night when most of the crew were ashore, and stowed deep in the ship, nailed down in a place where no one would know except the men who had put them there. They may have been purchased outright, or carried for commission to a pre-arranged buyer in Batavia. Once aboard, the men concerned would have denied any knowledge of them until the business at the other

54

end had been completed in equal secrecy and it was safe to move the ivory.

But the tusks never reached their destination, and it was to be another 240 years before they were handled by men again. Their value was by then long lost to the ivory carvers of Indonesia, China, or Japan, or to their lamenting owners —who were almost certainly Jan Steyns and Jan Nebbens.

Though by Company regulations the *Zeewyk* was allowed only twenty days at the Cape, none of the crew complained when she stayed an extra six. It was not until 21 April that she raised her anchors and sailed out of Table Bay into the East. Her time was running out, and so were the spans of many of the 158 men still left aboard.

In the great cabin, Jan Steyns had rolled and put away the Company charts and instructions for the Atlantic. As the *Zeewyk* lifted to the ocean swells, he read again the familiar words of the Indian Ocean Sailing Orders:

The Cape of Good Hope being doubled it is thought good that you sail in an Easterly direction between 36 deg. and 39 deg. South Latitude, until you have reached a point 800 mylen (Holland miles, each the equivalent of $3\frac{1}{2}$ English statute miles) E. of the Cape of Good Hope; that you then direct your course as much N. as E. in such a manner that on reaching 30 deg. S. Lat. you should find yourself 950 or 1000 mylen (3,000 miles) from the Cape of Good Hope.

These 950 or 1,000 mylen being attained it is advisable, wind and weather permitting, that you bear down on the Land of Eendracht at 27 deg., or more to the N. as will enable you to clear the Tryall shoals lying about 20 deg. S. Lat., without danger and to touch the South coast of Java with ease in order to have the weather gauge of the Straits of Sunda, and reach these straits without loss of time. It must be understood that this is about the time when the East Monsoon blows south of the Line, and that the 950 or 1,000 mylen may be reached between the beginning of March and the end of September.

This was clear and unequivocal, as were most of the

Company instructions, and was followed by a cautionary note:

> Observe that the distance between the Cape and the Land of Eendracht is in reality much shorter than the chart shows, and it may happen by the aid of currents that the route may be found even shorter than it really is. So that the Land may be reached in much less time than we are led to expect.
> Remember that the Land of Eendracht S. of 27 deg. Lat. has many perilous sandbanks and that the soundings are of sharp rocks, consequently EXTREME CAUTION and the constant use of the lead at night and in stormy weather is indispensably necessary. . . .

Steyns was to have a good deal of time to remember that last paragraph. The Company never forgot it.

His eyes flicked over the Mercator chart. The ragged line of coast. The names of wrecks and dead men. The soundings of reef and shoal . . . perilous sandbanks . . . soundings of sharp rocks . . .

On 31 May a curious entry was recorded in the daily register. ". . . It was unanimously decided to steer ENE, if there is an opportunity and if it is feasible, to call at the Land of Eendracht."

With that entry, recorded without reason or explanation for this decision of the ship's council, the fate of the *Zeewyk* and her men was sealed.

The Land of Eendracht!

6
The Devil's Own

THE GRIM COAST OF EENDRACHT LAY WAITING FOR THEM AT the bottom of the world.

Australia of the future, as yet unnamed. A vast primaeval continent, sprawling asleep among uncharted seas south of the Equator. Terra Incognita, the unknown land. Brooding, hostile.

No one knew what lay behind the coastal hills which backed the sand-dunes of the forbidding shore. The exploration parties all gave up a few miles inland. Heat, dust, flies, a few miserably naked blacks, sun-shimmering distances . . . the reports were universally depressing.

The off-shore reefs were notorious for shipwreck. It was true that by 1727 no one aboard Dutch ships paid much credence to the old superstitions about whirlpools and dragons. But the Indonesians still firmly believed in the Garuda bird, a winged giant with iron talons which could carry off a Java rhinoceros, or a buffalo, and pluck men from the decks of ships. They said it nested in the region of Australia.

The Arab dhow traders told of a lost Austral region they called the Mohit. A dismal plant called the Wak Wak tree grew there, with hanging fruit in the shape of human skulls which used to cry out "Wak! Wak!" in doleful tones when they fell to the ground.

To the hardheaded Dutch the Western Australian coast, which they called the Land of Eendracht or Zuytlandt, the Southland, was simply a very long and dangerous coast. Useless for trade and responsible for grievous losses of ships and men, its unprofitable bulk blocked the passage of ships from the Indies to the Pacific below New Guinea. If, through some gigantic tremor of the earth, it had sunk below the waves forever, they would have rejoiced exceedingly. Since it was a hazard on the edge of their sea route to the Indies they recognized it in their sailing directions as a nuisance and a peril. Nothing more. There was no thought of making a territorial claim, because there was nothing there which to Dutch eyes appeared to justify the expenditure of even a few guilders for a solitary flag on a pole. The world was full of empty lands in the 1600s and 1700s.

The clear instruction to skippers of VOC ships sailing to the Indies was to keep away from the coast of Eendracht below twenty-seven degrees, South Latitude, the region of the wrecks. Jan Steyns' extraordinary proposed course was taking him in to meet that coast at twenty-nine degrees, nearly 140 miles inside the prohibited area, in waters forbidden to Indiamen for excellent reasons.

In the fourteen years before the *Zeewyk* sailed, three ships had been lost off the Zuytlandt coast. The *Zuytdorp* in 1712, the *Fortuyn* in 1724, and the *Aagtekerke* in 1726.

The Company sent no search ships to look for any of them, despite the fact that each of the ships had been carrying 250,000 guilders or more in silver and gold coin, and valuable cargoes in their holds. Too many expeditions had gone to the Southland coast in past years to search for wrecks and survivors, with dismal results. The searches had been nearly always unsuccessful, and invariably expensive. Often enough they had involved further losses of ships' boats and crews from the searching vessels.

58

Though no search vessels sailed for missing men and ships in the 1700s, there were survivors who reached the shore. Through the years, many castaway Dutchmen perished miserably on the Southland coast. There were some poignant stories.

Seven men from the ship *Vergulde Draeck* arrived at Batavia on 7 June 1656, to report that their ship had been wrecked on the Southland with 118 people drowned and sixty-eight still marooned on the coast, awaiting rescue. Ships were sent at once, but the search was hampered by bad weather and the survivors could not be found. Three successive expeditions failed to find anything more than scattered wreckage and a circle of planks on the beach which may have been a frame for a wreck-sail tent. The people were presumed to have wandered away or been murdered by Aborigines. Skeletons and coins from the wreck have been found on shore in our own century, and many pieces of eight and elephant tusks recovered from the wreck, which was discovered by divers in 1963.

The *Zuytdorp* crew struggled up steep red cliffs from the wreck of their ship in 1712. They lit huge bonfires of barrels and broken chests on the cliff-top in the hope that the flames or smoke might be seen by a passing ship. But no-one saw the fires, or, if they did, must have ascribed them to natives.

The *Zuytdorp* men died. The ashes of their fires, with ship nails, chest hinges, and barrel rungs, remain on that coast today. So do fragments of glass, where they smashed gin and brandy bottles on the rocks in a last despairing drunken spree. The silver coins from her treasure chests lie welded by corrosion to the sea-bed, in solid lumps protected by a huge surf which roars and thunders over her sea grave.

Men from the *Fortuyn* or *Aagtekerke* got ashore on the southern Abrolhos Islands in the 1720s. They dug wells in search of water but, like the others, Eendracht swallowed them up in the end.

The most horrifying shipwreck of them all was that of the *Batavia*, in 1629.

She was a new ship flying the pennants of her maiden

voyage when she sailed from Amsterdam in October, 1628. She was named after the new Indies capital of the East India Company, and had aboard 316 seamen, soldiers, VOC clerks and officials, as well as women and children. In the strong-room was a treasure of 250,000 guilders in twelve chests of coins, as well as jewels and precious goods themselves worth a king's ransom.

Things went badly with her from the start. The commander of the vessel, and president of the 1628 October Indies fleet, was the senior merchant, Francisco Pelsaert. The Vereenigde Oost-Indische Compagnie at this period customarily placed a merchant in charge of important ships. The merchant sailed as administrator, in a position of overall command, while the skipper of the vessel was in charge of the handling of the ship under his direction.

The skippers not unnaturally tended to resent taking orders from landsmen, and the skipper of the *Batavia*—a roughneck called Ariaen Jacobsz—was already an old enemy of Pelsaert. They had quarrelled at the Indian port of Surat in a previous year, when Pelsaert was an official of lesser importance and Jacobsz was skipper of the ship *Dordrecht*. When Pelsaert was elevated above Jacobsz' head, in command of both him and his new ship, the skipper grudged the merchant's every word and gesture of authority.

Pelsaert exercised his seniority to the full. When Jacobsz became involved in a drunken brawl aboard the warship *Buren* at the Cape of Good Hope, behaving "very beastly with words as well as deeds," he threatened to have him dismissed from his post. There was also a young and attractive woman, Lucretia van der Mylen, travelling to join her husband in the Indies. Jacobsz lusted after her, but she peremptorily rejected his advances and hurt his pride. Since he could not have her, and by way of revenge, he seduced her serving maid.

It is probable that Pelsaert himself was interested in Lucretia, and she may have been a further cause of the deep hatred between the commander and his skipper. The third figure in the events which were about to unfold was the sinister, scheming undermerchant, Jeronimus Cornelisz, a former apothecary from Haarlem. He also desired the beautiful Lucretia.

On the easting run from the Cape of Good Hope across the Indian Ocean, relations between Pelsaert and Jacobsz reached a critical point. After one stormy interview, Jacobsz declared that he was ready to mutiny and throw Pelsaert overboard. Cornelisz, the undermerchant, encouraged his resentment with sly malice. The mutiny plot passed from the stage of being a resentful drunken threat over a bottle of brandy to a serious intention. There was little difficulty in recruiting cut-throats from among the brutal soldiers, sailors, and gunners for'ard. Every Indiaman carried her share of men who would murder their mothers for a Rix dollar, and the *Batavia* had treasure enough aboard to tempt any mutineer. She was a rich prize as a vessel in herself, and there were also the women—all the ingredients to beckon the hell-rakers, the gold-hungry, the rapists, the murderers.

The mutineers decided to provoke Pelsaert to unpopular disciplinary measures by an outrage against Lucretia. They jumped on her in the dusk, stripped her naked, and smeared her with excreta and pitch. Despite their cloaked disguises she recognized some of their voices, and Pelsaert planned to arrest the ring-leaders on the day the lookouts sighted the Southland. He did not know that the arrests were to be the signal for the outbreak of mutiny.

Jacobsz and Cornelisz planned to take the *Batavia* pirating on the Barbary and African coasts, after killing all the officers and any members of the çrew who persisted in misguided loyalty to the Company.

But before the coast of Eendracht was sighted the *Batavia* ran on to an outlying coral reef of the Abrolhos Islands, forty miles from the mainland, in the darkness before dawn. The lookouts mistook the surf for moonlight on the water and before the helmsman could swing hard over she was aground in breaking surf.

In a few hours the ship was breached, and flooded, and all aboard could see that she was doomed. The passengers were put ashore on islands which Pelsaert described in his journal as being miserable ground little better than half-tide banks.

There were only two ship's boats, and very little food and water for the mass of weeping, praying, "poor-hearted" men and women dumped on the cold rocks of the islands. The officers and seamen, Pelsaert among them, camped on a separate island with the boats.

On the morning of the second day after the wreck the largest boat with Pelsaert, Jacobsz, and the officers had gone. A note left under a barrel said that they had left to search for water on the islands, and if none could be found there they would sail to the Southland mainland. They promised to return. The second boat, with the remainder of the seamen and officers, followed next day.

The passengers cried that they had been deserted; abandoned to die of thirst and starvation. Seventy-five men left out on the wreck, which was fast breaking up under their feet, had similar bitter thoughts.

Despite the promises the boats never came back, and the castaways were left to work out their own salvation. Afterwards, Pelsaert always maintained that he had intended to return. "Better and more honest to die with them if we did not find it (water) than to stay alive with deep grief of heart," he wrote in his journal. But the men in the boats were frightened. They could smell death on the islands. They failed to find water on the Abrolhos, though there was good water on both the large islands of the group, and it is questionable how hard they looked. According to Pelsaert's journal they then unanimously decided to sail with both boats to the mainland. It is doubtful that the seamen, who were realists and knew the odds against them, really intended to come back. After abandoning the smaller boat the party, which by this time totalled forty-six people—including a woman with a baby at breast—sailed north for Batavia and arrived off Java on 3 July 1629.

Governor Jan Pieterzoon Coen received them coldly. He ordered Pelsaert to return immediately, in the little vessel *Sardam*, "To the place where you have lost the ship and left the people."

He had skipper Ariaen Jacobsz flung into the dungeons on a charge of losing the ship by negligent navigation. The High Boatswain, Jan Evertsz, named by Pelsaert in his report as one of the men involved in the shipboard outrage against Lucretia van der Mylen, was hanged on the gallows out of hand.

Should Pelsaert have gone on to Batavia, or should he have returned to the islands with the smaller boat to keep order and maintain morale among the castaways? It is a difficult question to answer three centuries later. But the poor leaderless people on the island were left with less food and water for 180 people than was taken by the forty-six in the two boats. There were also the men and the Company's treasure stranded on the disintegrating wreck and left to the mercy of the waves.

The senior councillor (later governor) at Batavia, Antonie van Diemen, described the ship and passengers as "shamefully left."

In fact the people on the islands very nearly died. They were reduced to drinking their own urine, and some of the weaker ones were dead when the main body were saved by a fortunate shower of rain. Forty of the men on the ship died in an effort to reach the shore. But those who survived the despair of the first few days were able to make driftwood rafts to reach other islands, and they discovered eggs, birds, and other natural food on the coral cays. They made water catchments from sail-tents to fill water barrels, and gradually settled into a Robinson Crusoe existence.

Jeronimus Cornelisz was the last to leave the ship, floating ashore with a spar on 12 June, and as undermerchant he found himself the senior remaining VOC official. He assumed command of the castaways, but if he felt pleased by his new importance his peace of mind was shattered when he learnt that one of the men involved in the mutiny plot, the gunner Ryckert Wouters, had blabbed in a drunken moment. The story—or enough of it to have them all tortured and hanged if they should ever reach Batavia—was rife through the camp. He and a nucleus of plotters decided to go through with the mutiny on the islands and to seize the rescue ship. She would make a less impressive pirate than the splendid *Batavia*, but after all they had no choice. The mutineers, about thirty in all, began secretly and systematically murdering men, women, and children. Though they were outnumbered at first they had the advantage that Cornelisz, as senior officer of the castaways, had taken all the arms in custody, and had dispersed the people in isolated groups over several islands. The well-armed mutineers took the defenceless groups one by one, and killed more than a hundred of them in frightful fashion. By drowning, throat-cutting, and beating on the head with bloody clubs, stabbing through with pikes, or hacking about the head and neck with swords. Skulls still found on the islands show the marks of the weapons and the animal ferocity of the attackers. Once they had gained superiority, they kept on murdering for the blood-lust pleasure of it; amusements like cutting off the head of a young boy, Cornelis Aldersz, to see whether it could be done with one stroke of a sword. Or the ceremonial murder of the barber, Fransz Jansz, with three weapons; morningstar club, pike, and sword. They broke six knives in pieces on one poor carpenter, Jacop Hendrix Drayer, before cutting his throat with a fragment of broken steel. Babies and pregnant women were dispatched with clubs and adzes as brutally and mercilessly as they slew boys and grown men. They killed like a wolf pack among a flock of trapped sheep, only stopping, gore-stained, panting, when there were no more left to slaughter.

Jeronimus Cornelisz elected himself Captain-General, and had his adherents swear a curious oath of loyalty. "So truly as God shall help us and will take the same (oath) on the salvation of our souls to be faithful to each other in everything."

It is hard to imagine that after what they had done they could believe any of their souls might be considered for salvation. But they signed the documents solemnly.

They also fixed their signatures and marks, in the candlelight of Cornelisz' tent, to an oath to "Accept as our chief and Captain-General Jeronimus Cornelisz whom we with one accord and each separately swear so truly as God shall help us to be faithful and obedient in all that he shall order us. And in so far as the contrary happens we shall be the Devil's own . . . This Done on the Island of Batavia's Graveyard, August 20, 1629."

The Devil's Own—that was more like it.

Jeronimus opened the Company's chests brought ashore from the wreck and gave rich clothes to his followers. He "Gave free reign to his pride and devilish arrogance on these poor miserable islands. More by changing daily into different clothes, silk stockings with gold lace. To all his followers whom he could best trust, he gave clothes made from red cloth sewn with two or more bands of gold trimmings. And created a new mode of cassock, believing such vain and evil pleasures could last for ever!"

The quiver of indignation in Pelsaert's pen, as he wrote of the red cassocks and gold trimmings clothing the gross bodies of the mutineers, survives three centuries.

It shows the great gap between his time and our own. Today the foolish fopperies of the mutineers, their petty larceny with the tinselled cloth, would have passed almost unnoticed against the blood of the maimed and murdered passengers. But in Pelsaert's day life was cheaper, and property—particularly that of the VOC—was sacrosanct.

Of course they raped the women. The better looking and youngest were parcelled out among the mutineers, to do whatever was willed of them. Those who resisted had their throats cut, and the poor unwanted women had no chance at all. Jeronimus selected Lucretia van der Mylen for his own concubine. It was his vanity that he would win her with charm and persuasion. He had moved in artists' circles in Haarlem. She wept in his tent for twelve days before succumbing, and her surrender was only achieved when David Seevnack, one of the most notorious murderers, whispered venomously in her ear that she would have her throat cut like the others unless she pleased the Captain-General better. She gave in to him that day.

With salvaged butts of Spanish wine, chests of brocade, the barrels of provisions which washed in from the wreck, the jewels and the lighter treasures brought ashore by

Pelsaert before the boats departed, the mutineers were crowing cocks of their little row. Lords of the crabs and seagulls on their tiny island, in their dreams there was no limit to their future wealth and domains.

However, they admitted to having one problem. They had got rid of a band of soldiers, before the general massacre, by setting them ashore on a large island. The mutineers believed it to be waterless, but tricked the troops into making a new search—promising, of course, to return and take them off again. The plan was to leave the soldiers there to die bloodlessly of thirst, but, under a man named Weibbe Hayes, they found water in unsuspected places, as well as birds, eggs, and a species of small wallaby which could be caught and roasted. They had not only survived, they were living even better than the mutineers.

The soldiers were joined by refugees from the massacres on the islands near the wreck, and eventually their group numbered nearly forty. Though they posed no direct threat to the better-armed mutineers, there was the chance that they might warn the rescue ship when it arrived.

So it was decided to massacre them, which was not expected to be difficult because the soldiers had been unarmed. A boatload of mutineers swaggered across to the large island in their fine red coats for a little sporting throat-cutting, but the soldiers, under the determined and resourceful Weibbe Hayes, proved a far tougher proposition than pregnant women and young boys. Warned of the massacres on the other islands, and expecting a visit from the mutineers, they had made improvised pikes from wreck wood and pieces of sharpened barrel-hoop. They defended themselves stoutly, and though there were casualties on both sides the mutineers had the worst of the early encounters. Their leaders were killed or taken prisoner, and a pitched battle was raging on 17 September 1629, the day the rescue ship dropped anchor. There was a race to warn the ship, won by Weibbe Hayes. The mutineers, cowed by the sight of the *Sardam's* cannon, lapsed into sullen cowardice and surrendered without firing a shot.

Forlorn now in their finery they were taken and chained

and their interrogation by torture began at once. Pelsaert employed the water cure, an old favourite in the East and used as recently as 1943 and 1944 by the Japanese in Asian prisoner of war camps.

Canvas was tied around the subject's neck so that water could not escape, and it was as though his head were in the bottom of a bucket. Water was then poured until the level rose above his nostrils and he had to lower the level by drinking in order to breath. As he drank more water was poured. He gasped and swallowed, and bubbled, and breathed, choked and cursed, and drank more and more. Finally his stomach seemed at splitting point, hideously distended, and he lost control of his bowels and bladder. It was unendurable.

But still the torturers poured until, in the agony of bursting and suffocation, he told them what they wanted. Under Dutch law a man could only be sentenced to death on his own confession, and he must sign to confirm the confession again of his own free will without duress 24 hours after being tortured. Of course if he changed his mind and recanted they tortured him again. And again. Until they were satisfied they had the truth of the matter.

Confessions of the mutineers were checked against each other until they matched in horrid detail and the guilt was clearly established. The question was whether to ship them back to Batavia in chains for formal and elaborate execution, or hang them on the spot.

Pelsaert was worried because the *Sardam* had only thirty men. Some of them were divers, and these had succeeded in raising ten of the twelve chests of treasure from the wreck. Unexpected good fortune. But so much wealth so close and so weakly defended was too much temptation for a company containing "many corrupt and half-corrupted people." One mutiny was more than enough. He feared the persuasive tongue of Jeronimus Cornelisz, architect of all previous evils, whose sly whispers still reached the ears of the camp despite the guard mounted over him.

Pelsaert decided to hang Cornelisz and the ring-leaders, and take the lesser villains back to Batavia Castle for trial.

Sentence was passed on 28 September. Jeronimus Cornelisz, "Besmirched not only with abominable misdeeds but also with damnable heresy, declaring that there is neither Devil nor Hell, and has tried to imprint this into the people on this island—moreover that it is still his daily work to bring with his tongue well-intentioned people to a wrong opinion and lead them from the straight path . . ."

He was sentenced to have both his hands chopped off at the wrists and to be hanged: "Punished by the cord at the gallows." Jan Hendricxsz of Bremen, soldier, aged 21 years; Lenart Michielsz van Os, cadet, 21 years; Mattys Beer, of Munsterbergh, soldier, 21 years; Allert Jansz of Assendelft, gunner, aged 24 years; were all sentenced to have their right hands cut off and also be hanged.

Andries Jonas, soldier, aged about 40; Rutger Frericxz, of Groeningen, locksmith, 23 years; and Jan Pelgrom, steward, of Bemel, 18 years, were to be hanged without mutilation.

Their confessions, still preserved in The Hague in the journal of Francisco Pelsaert, show the horror of those days on the coral cays. The examination, confession, and sentence of Jan Hendricxsz was typical of the confessions Pelsaert extracted from the mutineers. A testimony of blood and terror which tells its own tale better than any description.

Today 17 Sept. in the afternoon, on the ship SARDAM, *has been resolved by the Commandeur* FRANCO. PELSART *and the ship's council, to examine Jan Hendricx of Bremen on the great murders so understood to have done, and, if necessary, to bring him to torture— date as before.*

Jan Hendricxsz of Bremen, soldier, aged about 24 years, brought in, is asked by the Commandeur why they had wanted to seize the ship; answered, free and unbound, without torture, that over 6 weeks (ago) Jeronimus Cornelisz, under-merchant, and his council had taken that plan and sworn to make themselves masters of the first Yacht that should come; but that he is innocent of that and in no way consented to it, though several times was requested about it.

And in order to come to the straight truth of it, is put to torture.

Has promised of his own freewill to say what he knows. Says, that he was persuaded thereto, as well as (were) all persons who were on the island; the Commandeur asked him again why he wanted to do that; answered, that he did not know. Furthermore examined how they would have brought it about, says, that already before Jeronimus had been captured by the other party, they had had the plan, if a Yacht should come, to let the boat come to land first and then make the crew drunk in order the easier to kill them, and they should then have mastered the yacht easily at night time, with the boat, because they guessed that there would only be 20 to 30 Men. But no decision was yet taken as to how they would begin it, because while they were fighting with the other party, they suddenly saw the ship.

He, further examined as to where they would have sailed had they seized it, and how many people would have been left alive, answered, that the plan was to run off to Spain, Barbary or such-like places in order to sell the ship and share the booty; that they would have spared the lives of the skipper, the steersman, with 5 or 6 of the sailors who would serve them but would have murdered the rest.

Further examined as to how many people he has murdered; whereto confesses of freewill that he has killed 18 to 20 by the order of Jeronimus, but that he did not know their names, therefore requested respite till the following day, in order to bethink himself how and when he has done all this; which is allowed.

On 19 do. on the Island BATAVIA'S GRAVEYARD, *before the ship's council,*

Jan Hendricxsz, before mentioned, called again and being asked by the Commandeur if he would have been one of the conspirators in the seizing of the ship *Batavia*, says, that he was not one of them, and has not been one on the Ship, but that he had heard from several persons (now all dead) that the skipper (Ariaen Jacobsz), Jeronimus, High boatswain (Jan Evertsz), Ryckert Woutersz gunner, Allert Jansz of Assendelft, gunner, Coenraat van Huyssen and

Gysbert van Welderen, soldiers, with about 10 to 12 others, had undertaken this first and had made the plan to nail the soldiers' Hatch at night, until they had become masters of the ship. Then they would have chosen those of the soldiers who were on their side, but the rest they would have murdered, all except about 120. Said also that he knew Allert Jansz of Assendelft was one of the accomplices.

Towards evening he has been called again and asked if he has now remembered how many people he has murdered. Confesses as follows:—

That he one day (being 5 July last), together with Davidt van Sevanck, Coenraat van Huyssen, Cornelis, Mattys Beer, Lenert Michielsz and Wouter Loos, were ordered by Jeronimus to go with the biggest Raft, and that they should take with them and drown Hans Radder, cadet, and Jacop Groenewald, upper trumpeter; whom he has helped to bind hand and foot, and in that way (they) have been drowned.

Confesses further that on the day (being the 9 July last) he was ordered by Jeronimus, together with Sevanck, Coenraat van Huyssen, Gysbrecht van Welderen, Jacob Pietersz *lanspesaat*, Lenert Michielsz and Lucas Jelisz, to go with the little yawl and do what Zevanck ordered them to do. They had then gone to where on another island (Traitor's Island), Pieter Jansz, provost, with his wife and child, Claas Harmansz of Maagdenburgh with his wife, Claudine Patoys with her child, Jacop Jacopsz, cooper; Pauwels Barentsz, Bessel Jansz, sailors; Cristoffel Quist of Rokema, soldier; Nicklaas Winckelhaack, soldier; pieters Arentsz of Monickendam, sailor; and Wouter Joel, *schotsman*, had made 2 small rafts with which they thought, according to a promise under oath which Jeronimus at that time had made, to sail to the High island; coming to them, they forced the men to jump from the rafts and help to push them further towards *Batavia's* island; when they came to the shallows Davidt Zevanck ran on the land to Jeronimus and asked him something, whereon Zevanck came back and called out: "Kill" at which Jan Hendricxsz did his utmost; but many escaped and thought to save themselves on the island by Jeronimus, but he ordered that they should be killed, and

Zevanck, with Coenraat van Huyssen and Gysbert van Welderen went in the same little yawl and took the three above mentioned women, who were still sitting on the Raft, and took them to the deep, where they were thrown overboard and drowned.

Item, confesses that one day the 8 July, he was ordered by Jeronimus, when Zevanck was by, to strangle the child of Hans Hardens, named Hilletgie, which he did while Jeronimus invited the mother.

Item, confesses that one day, being the 10 July last, together with Allert Jansz of Assendelft, gunner, he has cut the throat of Jan Piuten, English soldier.

Item, confesses that one day (being 12 July last) he was called by Jeronimus into his tent, together with Lenert Michielsz and Lucas Gellisz, and that they were ordered to cut the throats of Passchier van den Ende, gunner, Jacop Hendrix Drayer, carpenter (*timmerman*), and a sick cabin boy; whereupon he, together with Davidt Zevanck and others who were so ordered, took a lamp and went into their tent and asked Passchier if he had any goods hidden there, to say so. He answered weepingly, "No," and begged that he might be allowed to say his prayers, because he thought that it would cost him his life. But Zevanck said, "Get on with it." Thus Jan Hendricxsz threw him to the ground and cut his throat. The other one Jacop Hendrix Drayer begged bitterly for his life, whereupon Zevanck and they also went to Jeronimus and said that Jacop was a good carpenter and should he not be spared. But Jeronimus answered, "Not at all, he is only a turner, furthermore, he is half lame. He also must go. He might become a babbler now or later." Whereon they have gone back to the small tent and Jan Hendricxsz threw the foresaid Jacop to the ground and Lenert Michielsz sat on his body and Jan Hendricxsz stabbed 2 knives to pieces on his breast, also 2 knives on his throat, whereupon Lucas Gellisz handed him one of his knives, but he could not bring him to death, so that at last he cut his throat with a piece of knife; after that did likewise to the boy.

Item, confesses that one day (being 14 July last), he has been called by Jeronimus into his tent, together with Lenert

Michielsz and Rutger Fredericx, and that they were ordered to kill Andries de Vries, assistant — he gave them each a sword therefor, and poured each a beaker of wine; which they have done publicly.

Item, confesses that he one day (being 15 July last) has been fetched out of his tent by Jeronimus and ordered, together with Sevanck, Coenraat van Huyssen, Cornelis Pietersz of Utrecht, Hans Jacopsz of Basel and Mr Frans Jansz of Hoorn, barber, that they should go with the little yawl to Seals Island to kill all people there, about 40 altogether, of whom he, Jan Hendricxsz, as soon as they arrived, has killed 5 boys, and after that 2 Men, but he did not know their names. But Cornelis Jansz the assistant, with 3 to 4 others who were chased by Hans Jacopsz, escaped on rafts; and also at that time they spared the lives of 4 women, namely, Mayken Soers, Jannetgie Gist, Gertien Willemsz, widow, and Laurentia Thomasz; also some children were spared.

Item, confesses that he one day (being 21 July) has been called by Jeronimus into his tent, and that he gave him to know that at night time he must help with the murder of the Predikant's (preacher's) family, and that he must do that which Zevanck ordered him to do. At night, when Jeronimus, with the Predikant and his eldest daughter had been invited into the tent of Coenraat van Huyssen, then he, Jan Hendricxsz, with Zevanck, Wouter Loos, Cornelis Pietersz, Andries Liebent, Jacop Pietersz and Andries Jonas, have gone to the predikant's tent; Zevanck has called outside Wybrecht Claasen, a young girl, whom Jan Hendricxsz stabbed with a dagger, and inside, all people, the mother with 6 children, had their heads battered in with adzes, and so they were dragged into a hole·that had been made therefor.

Confesses also that on that night, after the foresaid woeful tragedy had been committed, he has battered in the head of Hendrick Denys of Amsterdam, assistant, with an adze, in front of his tent, so that he died immediately.

Item, furthermore confesses also that one day, being 28 July, he has been called by Jeronimus into his tent and ordered to take with him Andries Liebent and Jan van Bemel in order to strangle Anneken Hardens wife of Hans Hardens. Whereon he went into the tent; meanwhile Gysbrecht van Welderen came to help him, who made a halter out of her snood and with that strangled her.

On 28 do. before the Ship's Council,

Because Lucas Gellisz has been accused that he also has stabbed a knife to pieces on Jacop Hendrix, has been confronted with Jan Hendricxsz, whether he has seen that, and says that he himself (i.e., Jan Hendricxsz) has stabbed to pieces 4 knives on the mentioned man, but that Lucas has handed him his knife for that purpose.

Further, asked again if when a Yacht should have come and they should have come to the execution of their plan, he would have helped in the seizing of it, confesses, "Yea," for there were very few who would not have had a hand in it.

Item, confesses of freewill that he had been called one day (being 6 August last) by Jeronimus, who in the morning stood in the tent of Zevanck, and that he said to him, "Go and stab to the heart Stoffel Stoffelsz of Amsterdam, carpenter, that lazy dog who stands there working, for he is not worth his keep." And thereupon gave him his own dagger which he carried in his pocket. Whereon Jan Hendricxsz killed him with 2 blows.

Furthermore he declares, unasked, that he has brought to mind that one evening Jeronimus has invited him, together with Allert Janssen of Assendelft, and amongst other things he has told them that if the ship *Batavia* had not wrecked, they would shortly have seized it and so made themselves rich men;

. . . Also he has outraged the Women, as well as many misdeeds which it would seem have to remain hidden, Criminal offences which weight very heavily and which cannot be allowed to be suffered by God or mankind, as nature teaches us sufficiently that such evil-doers cannot as an example to others be allowed to remain unpunished. Therefore the Commandeur *Franco. pelsart* and we undersigned persons of the council of the ship *Sardam*, having

73

given the greatest attention to this matter, after long examinations and interrogations, having exchanged our thoughts with each other and weighed and pondered, in order to save ourselves from the wrath of God and to cleanse Christianity from such a villain—have sentenced the foresaid Jan Hendricxsz as we sentence him herewith, that he shall be taken on Monday the first of October 1629 to Seals Island, to a place made ready for that, to execute Justice, and there firstly to cut off his right hand and after that to punish him on a Gallows with the Cord till death shall follow, with confiscation of all his goods, kit, monthly wages and all that he may have to claim here in India against the General East India Company, our Lord Masters. Thus done and attested on the Island *Batavia's* Graveyard, this 28 September, Anno 1629.

> FranCo. Pelsartt
> Jacob Jacobs *houten man*
> Claas Gerritsz
> Jacop Jansz
> Sijmon Yopzoon
> *This is the mark of*
> Jan X Willemsz
> Visch

The executions, it was decided, were to be carried out on wreck-timber gallows on another island. They were delayed a day by bad weather, but eventually took place early on a cold drizzling morning, 2 October, 1629. They did not go smoothly, and the report states: "Coming there the condemned begged that Jeronimus should be hanged first so that their eyes could see that the seducer of men died. But Jeronimus could not reconcile himself to dying or to penitence, neither to pray to God nor to show any face of repentance over his sins. But they all shouted at each other 'Revenge!' . . . Some evil-doers shouted 'Revenge!' at Jeronimus, and he shouted at them. At last he challenged them as well as the Ship's Council before God's judgment seat that he would seek justice there because he had not been able to get it on earth."

Most of the cut-throats died on the gallows unrepentant.

But the eighth, the boy Jan Pelgrom who had been involved in some of the most brutal murdering of the hapless passengers, could not face his own death though he had exulted over others. He "wailed and pleaded for grace," imploring "That one should put him on an island, and let him live a little longer."

Sickened by the executions and hand choppings they flung him whimpering back into the boat, and as the *Sardam* sailed northwards cast him and a man called Wouter Looes adrift with a sampan, weapons, and trade goods, at a spot near the mouth of the present Murchison River. "Men's luck is found in strange places," Pelsaert told them, not unkindly, as they rowed away towards the shore. Australia's reluctant first white settlers, they vanished from history at that point.

The others, taken back in fetters by Pelsaert, must have wished later they could change places with Looes and Pelgrom and take their chance with the savages of the Southland. The Court in Batavia ordered ruthless punishments, including breaking on the wheel, hangings, and flogging on the neck, and most of them were executed.

Pelsaert himself was blamed by many of his contemporaries for the mutiny because he had left the people in a desperate and vulnerable situation with no senior officers. He should have sent the seamen for help and remained behind himself to keep order, they said, and — despite the impression one gets from Pelsaert's journal of a pleasant and gentle person — it is hard to disagree. Investigations were being made into his part in the voyage, the wreck, and the aftermath, when he forestalled judgment by dying in September, 1630. His health had been undermined by the long open boat voyage, and mental agony and guilt over the *Batavia* disaster. "Continuous grief and sorrow of the heart which can scarcely be forgotten or ignored by me. Yea, the pack of all disasters has moulded together and fallen on my neck . . ." he lamented in one of his last letters. His goods and wages were confiscated by the Company after his death, and the stigma of disgrace gathered over his name.

Weibbe Hayes, the brave leader of the soldiers, was

elevated from private to lieutenant with proportionate increase in pay, and was hailed rightly as a hero.

Lucretia van der Mylen, whose own account of the *Batavia* affair must surely have been the most interesting of all if she had ever kept one, lived on to be a very old lady.

The brawling skipper, Ariaen Jacobsz, was still in Batavia Castle dungeons two years after the wreck, and at that time was being put to the torture "On strong suspicion of having intended to run off with the ship *Batavia*." Subsequent records appear to have been lost, but it is not likely that he escaped the wrath of the Company for his part in the strange history of the *Batavia*.

Antonie van Diemen, at that time a young and influential councillor at Batavia, later to become one of the most powerful governors in VOC history (he sent Tasman on his great 1642 voyage to circumnavigate Australia) wrote to the Council of Seventeen, in Holland: "It is certain that a completely Godless and evil life has been conducted on the mentioned ship (*Batavia*) of which both the skipper and the President Pelsaert are greatly guilty. May the Almighty forgive their sin, and make good the damage to the Company."

God may have forgiven Pelsaert and Jacobsz, but the Dutch East India Company never did.

An interesting sidelight to the story is that a wonderful cameo—believed to have been carved in 312 A.D.—and an exquisite Byzantine agate vase were part of the *Batavia* treasure, and were pawed over and fondled by the mutineers in their tents on *Batavia's* Graveyard. The cameo today is in the Royal Coin Cabinet in The Hague, the vase in the Walters Art Gallery, Baltimore, U.S.A., both of them tangible, touchable links with that time of terror and tragedy—on the grim islands off the Australian shore.

It would be interesting to hear what they could tell us of the conversations of Jeronimus and his blood-thirsty crew over their flagons of wreck wine at night. Of Francisco Pelsaert, and Lucretia van der Mylen, who clung to her honour for twelve days. . . .

76

7
Land at the End of the World

THE ABROLHOS ISLANDS, WHERE THE *Batavia* WAS WRECKED and where the *Zeewyk* was now headed on a disaster course, were discovered in 1619, three years after the first sighting of the main Southland.

The discovery was accidental. It occurred for the same reason as the other sightings, strandings, and actual wrecks which followed, on the reef-toothed coast of the Great South Land.

The mariners could not tell, except by intelligent guess-work how far east of the Cape of Good Hope they had travelled, because they had no way of telling their longitude. The mechanics of their navigation may seem a little tedious, but they are so important in terms of the early discoveries and the wrecks, and to the *Zeewyk*'s own strange story, that they repay a little study.

A means of calculating latitude—the position of a ship in relation to a fixed point north or south—was established as early as 1478 by the Jewish-Portuguese astronomer Abraham Zacuto. Navigators knew that the sun at the equator shone from directly overhead, and that as they sailed away north or south it appeared lower in the sky each noon until at the Arctic in the winter it barely lipped the horizon at midday. By measuring the angle of the noonday sun with an instrument called an astrolabe, they were able to establish their distance north or south of the equator. Of course there were variations for summer and winter, but Zacuto's almanac gave a table of declinations for every day of the year.

By 1727, when Steyns squinted his midday sun-sightings along the arm of an instrument known as a backstaff— which succeeded the astrolabe and was the forerunner of the quadrant and sextant—Indiamen navigators were able to get their latitudes within four or five miles, which was close enough for any ordinary purposes.

But calculating their longitude—the position of a ship in relation to a fixed point east or west—had them completely stumped. It was possible to determine longitude on shore by observations of the moon and the behaviour of the planets and their satellites. But this required prolonged viewing through a large telescope from a stationary position. It was neither practical nor possible on the shifting, heaving, slippery deck of a ship at sea.

Ignorance of longitudinal positions cost many ships and many men. It so vexed the British Admiralty, among others, that in 1714 a Board of Longitude was established. It offered the then enormous sum of £20,000 reward for the first man to devise a practical means of establishing longitude at sea.

A Yorkshireman named John Harrison claimed the reward in 1735, with a hand-made watch of superlative design which he called a chronometer—literally "time-measurer." The crusty old sea-dogs on the Board were taken aback. They had rather hoped for some easy form of lunars or moon-sightings, and for nearly thirty years they found excuses for not testing Harrison's device. It was not until 1761 that his chronometer was tested, proven, and became the basis for the means of determining longitude at sea which has been used ever since.

The principle was very simple. If you took a fixed point on earth—Greenwich Observatory on the River Thames was the one selected—and travelled away from it east or west, sunrises and sunsets would come earlier or later depending upon whether you headed into the rising sun or away from it. Similarly the midday zenith would occur earlier or later, because there is actually a time lag of about one minute for every seventeen miles, and one hour for every 1,020 miles, or fifteen degrees of longitude, travelled east or west.

So that if you kept a watch set permanently on Greenwich time, and compared it with your midday sighting, the difference in hours or minutes between the two could be converted into miles travelled east or west. Longitude, in fact. Taken together with the latitude, the distance from the equator shown by the angle of the sun at the midday shot, the position of the ship could be established exactly among the grid of lines of latitude and longitude intersecting each other at right angles on the chart. The Mercator meridians are each one degree, sixty nautical miles, or sixty-eight land miles, apart.

All this was fine in theory, but until John Harrison perfected his chronometer there was no time-piece reliable enough to be used for navigating a ship at sea. A watch which gained or lost three seconds every day could cause an error of thirty miles in position after six weeks. An error of three minutes every day would be disastrous in a voyage which might take months.

So latitude was the seaman's blessing, and longitude—or the lack of it—his curse. Ships sailed without a longitude until well after 1761. The Dutch ships, prior to 1800, did not use any form of exact calculation for longitude. Even James Cook, on his first voyage to the Pacific which led to the discovery of the east coast of Australia in 1770, had no chronometer, though he used one on his later voyages.

Skippers used their own rough and ready methods to fill in the longitude gap. British seamen called it sailing by "dead reckoning"; a corruption of "ded. reckoning," from "deduced reckoning." Dead men and ships were too often the result. Their methods actually amounted to taking an educated guess.

They made calculations on the speed of their vessel and worked out the distance travelled in sea-miles by the number of days since they left the last port or sighted the last conspicuous land features. "Land-marks" were tremendously important to them for this reason, because they gave an exact position not possible at sea.

The Dutch gauged their speed by throwing wood chips over the side and timing how long they took to pass between two set marks cut into the gunwales. The British had a more sophisticated device called a chip-log. It was a triangular piece of wood which scooped water like a sea-anchor and remained stationary while the ship moved on. It was attached to a line whose length was marked by knots at set intervals of forty-two feet, or seven fathoms. As the line hissed over the side the ship's speed in "knots" was calculated. An official "knot" was the equivalent of a nautical mile, one-sixth of a degree of latitude or longitude, and equal to one and one-eighth land miles.

A dampness in the sand-glass timing devices, a badly coiled knot-line, contrary currents, storms, confusions in the darkness, all led to errors. Over several months of travelling across oceans as vast as the Atlantic or Indian, an accumulation of mistakes could mean an error of hundreds of miles in longitude calculations. When Ariaen Jacobsz wrecked the *Batavia*, he was 600 miles farther east than he thought he was.

In the circumstances it may seem surprising that any ship reached port at all, but skippers only used their longitude calculation as a rough guide of when they might expect to see land. They placed much more reliance for actual position on depth soundings made by dropping the lead line, and on natural phenomena. Changes in the colour of the sea, floating weed, cuttle-fish bones, and especially the varieties of seabirds found only near coasts, all told them when land was near.

Samples of the sea-bed, brought up sticking to tallow in the hollow of the sounding lead—sand, mud, weed, gravel, coral—were also important. Atlantic fishing skippers claimed to be able to tell which cod bank they were over by the taste of the mud.

The old skippers did amazingly well, out of sight of land for months at a time. Even with the most sophisticated direction-finding gear, the radar, sonar, radio-beams, and other marvellous mechanical aids of the twentieth century, ships are still wrecked today. There were many more wrecks in the 1600s and 1700s, but most skippers still reached their destinations.

However, there were some areas in the world where the difficulties were exceptional. The Indian Ocean was one of them. The course across it was mainly in an easterly or longitudinal direction which meant that the navigators had no accurate notion of how far they had travelled, other than in terms of days of sailing and rough guesses at their speed.

The coast of Eendracht, waiting hostile on the other side of the ocean, spread its reefs and hazards over more than 2,000 miles athwart the path of any Java-bound ship which sailed too far. Even after 1700 it was imperfectly charted, and—as the sailing instructions warned—there were many off-shore reefs and sandbanks which reached for ship's keels.

It was a low-lying land, and ships came upon it without warning. Vessels reaching its longitude in fog, or blinded by rain squalls, or in the night, were in gravest peril.

It was called the Land of d'Eendracht by the Dutch after the vessel *Eendracht*, skipper Dirk Hartog of Amsterdam, merchant Gillies Miebais of Liege, which first raised the new land on 25 October 1616.

It was not the first sighting of the Australian continent— a vessel called the *Duyfken* had touched at the portion of Australia nearest New Guinea, in 1606—but it was the first landfall on the western coast. Discovery of the east coast was to wait until James Cook sighted it in 1770, more than a century and a half later.

The Portuguese route to the Indies sent their carracks crawling up the fever coast of Africa, following the old monsoon track of the Arab dhows. In fact it was a dhow navigator who originally showed Vasco da Gama the way to India. The Portuguese built forts along the route, and followed the same course for a century. But the deep-water Dutch and English sailors disliked the proximity of coasts and preferred the freedom of the open sea where winds were more consistent, voyages were faster, and they believed the air was purer and less noxious with fevers and pestilences.

Henrik Brouwer's accidental discovery of a belt of consistent westerly winds, in the Roaring Forties, made him sail in a half-circle and cover many more miles than on a direct course, but he made much faster time, because he avoided the notorious calms and fluky winds in the tropical centre of the Indian Ocean.

Soon all the Indiamen were following Brouwer's route, and it was only a matter of time before one went farther than the rest and the surprised skipper found Australia before his bows. Dirk Hartog was the man. The forty-mile-long island which forms one arm of Shark Bay, in Western Australia, is named after him. He left a pewter plate, with a scratched inscription to mark his landfall, nailed on a post on a high cliff. Ironically the first name on the plate was that of the merchant Gillies Miebais of Liege, who by VOC tradition of the early 1600s must have been the senior man aboard at the time. They did not name the new land, but humbly left this privilege to their Lords the Seventeen, the Directors of the VOC, who apparently did not think the discovery important enough to merit a name. So following captains called it Eendracht Landt, and in later years, when a name was given to the island, skippers had superseded merchants in VOC importance and Dirk Hartog was immortalised. Gillies Miebais has been forgotten in history, except as one of the names on Hartog's plate.

Soon other vessels were reporting Southland sightings, and by 1620 contacts were commonplace. The first wreck, that of the English ship *Tryall*, which tried to follow the Dutch route and lost her way, occurred in 1622. The *Batavia* followed in 1629, after a number of near misses by single ships and whole fleets of VOC Indiamen.

One of these occurred in July, 1619. A fleet commanded by Frederick Houtman, aboard the *Dordrecht*. "Deeming ourselves to be in the open sea . . . at night, about three hours before daybreak we came unexpectedly upon a low-lying coast. A level country with reefs all around it. We saw no high land or mainland, so that this shoal is to be very carefully avoided as it is very dangerous to ships that wish to touch at this coast . . ."

In this way the islands which play so large a part in our story were discovered. The Dutch called them Houtman's Abrolhos. Abrolhos was a traditional name for a dangerous coast, shoal, point, or rocky projection. It may have come from a corruption of the old Portuguese Lookout's cry "*Abri vossos olhos!* . . . Open your eyes! . . . Look out!" Some island shoals off the coast of Brazil were also called Abrolhos. There was a Point Abrojos on the Pacific coast of Mexico, and doubtless others where Portuguese, Spanish, and Dutch mariners sailed their ships around the world, like the numerous uses of such names as Wreck Point, Wreck Reef, and Point Danger on modern charts.

Few island shoals were more dangerous than Houtman's Abrolhos. The ships coming on them were sailing east or north-east. They had no longitude and were unsure of their positions. The islands were only a few feet above sea-level and were hard to see. The reefs stretched over nearly a full degree of longitude. When Governor Jan Pieterszoon Coen was nearly wrecked on them in September, 1627, he wrote, "We were at less than half a mile's distance from the breakers before we perceived them, without being able to see land. If we had come upon this place in the night time we should have been in a thousand perils with our ships and crews!"

It was a good description—Coen's alarm is still vivid after 343 years—and it was as a result of his experience that vessels were ordered to keep away from the Land of Eendracht south of twenty-seven degrees. Nevertheless ships were to be wrecked there, and at other points along the Southland coast.

As they were wrecked, and as expeditions were sent to look for them, the chart of the Southland was gradually filled in. Pelsaert's open boat voyage contributed some knowledge. Tasman, ordered to chart the north-west coast and to visit the Abrolhos to see whether he could salvage a *Batavia* treasure chest jammed against the rocks by a cannon, sailed as far as Willem's River (Exmouth Gulf of the future) before turning away in 1644. There were expeditions to search for the treasure and survivors of the *Gilt Dragon* in 1656, 1657, and 1658, all of which added knowledge even if the hope of saving life and salvaging treasure proved fruitless. In 1696 a major expedition of three ships, under the command of Willem de Vlamingh in the *Geelvinck*, was sent to the Southland to search for the remains of a ship called the *Ridderschap van Holland*. The expedition discovered the Swan River, charted Rottnest Island, and explored and mapped the coast north as far as Tasman's turn-off point at Exmouth Gulf. This virtually filled in the chart of the west of the Australian continent so far as the Dutch were concerned, and Vlamingh's chart became their official guide.

Steyns had Vlamingh's chart among the others in his cabin. He did not know that there· was one important omission—the Abrolhos. In sailing up the coast, de Vlamingh passed between the islands and the mainland. He did not sight the Abrolhos and consequently they were not recorded on his chart, except as a series of vague dots which did not reach as far south as twenty-nine degrees where the bow of the *Zeewyk* was pointed in June of 1727, "To call, if feasible, at the Land of Eendracht," as the journal entry of 31 May had it.

Why?

The sailing instructions left no room for doubt, saying, "Remember that the Land of Eendracht has south of twenty-seven degrees many perilous sandbanks and that the soundings are of sharp rocks."

What could have persuaded Jan Steyns, a new skipper with a new ship, to deliberately place his vessel, treasure, cargo, and crew, in peril? To steer his *Zeewyk* into the ship-trap of the Southland coast against his orders, and in the face of the sad experience of the previous shipwrecks?

There was no merit to be gained in exploration, for the coast had been sailed by ships looking for wreck survivors. There was no trade to be gained on that barren coast, as had

---

Top: When under full sail, an Indiaman of the *Zeewyk* class would look "as large as a block of flats" on the horizon. Bottom: The ornate figurehead, in this case the Lion of Zeeland, and heavily gilded scrollwork, were features of Dutch East Indiamen

been proved in the past by Dutchmen who had landed there. His ship was not disabled. It was not short of water or supplies.

Yet Steyns sailed the *Zeewyk* onwards on a course which could only lead them into hazard if he persisted—unless he turned away at the last moment, and abandoned his foolish plan.

There was still time . . .

8
How Better
to Die?

On Sunday, 8 June 1727, a fine clear day, the men on the *Zeewyk* saw new kinds of sea birds wheeling over the waves.

On the long run from the Cape, in cold southern latitudes with the boisterous westerly winds shrieking in the tautened rigging, albatrosses and giant black storm petrels had been a familiar sight, riding above the storm waves on seven to twelve foot wingspans, soaring and swooping like spirits on the wind.

Once the *Zeewyk* changed her course to north-east, and climbed back into warmer latitudes, their albatross friends left them. For a while they had seen no birds at all.

Now the new birds—"spotted gulls," as van der Graeff called them—and sunshine brought smiles to the faces of some of the new hands on deck, but the experienced sailors, those who had sailed to the Indies before, frowned when they saw them.

These birds meant land. Land not too far over the horizon, and in these latitudes it could only be the Southland or its out-riding reefs and islands.

The helmsmen looked questioningly for orders. But the course remained steadfast at east-north-east, as it had since 31 May, when the Ship's Council dominated by the skipper had made that strange decision. "If there is an opportunity . . . to call at the Land of Eendracht."

On 8 June they compensated the compasses "from 10 to 5 degrees E the needle," and the military sergeant named Christoffel Frank from Venlo died. Van der Graeff punctiliously recorded his spotted gull sighting. They buried the sergeant, as they had buried the other men— eleven in the month of May alone—sewn in his canvas shroud with a cannon ball under his stiffened toes. The prayer-book snapped shut on the familiar phrases of the burial service as his mortal remains slipped into the wake alongside the ship and were lost in the swirl of her passing. Astern of them the fins of the ship-following sharks lost station and disappeared.

They estimated twenty-one miles sailing that day, with an observed noon latitude of thirty degrees fifteen minutes and an estimated longitude of 123 degrees twenty-six minutes. The latitude was accurate, but their longitude estimation was hundreds of miles in error. Wind and current, the following seas of the southern latitudes, had deceived them, as they had deceived many others. And all day on 9 June, they sailed like Fredrik Houtman in 1619. He might have written his own lines for the *Zeewyk*. "Deeming ourselves to be in the open sea, we shaped our course North by East . . ."

Her noon Latitude of twenty-nine degrees six minutes was a mere six nautical miles, or slightly less than seven statute miles, below the southern tip of the Abrolhos archipelago. The birds which flew around and above her that day must have been able to see the ship and at the same time the islands to which she appeared inexorably drawn— the drama unfolding below, with the white teeth of surf on the waiting reef. . . .

The men on the ship, of course, were unaware. A heavy threatening sky, to the north, and showers during the afternoon, had reduced their visibility. The seamen on the yards who had clambered aloft to reef the topsails saw nothing out of the ordinary ahead of them, or they would have remarked on it.

Steyns must have pondered his charts again, considering his landfall, where he intended to fall in with the Southland main, and what his approach should be. Most previous sightings of the Abrolhos had been in twenty-eight degrees thirty minutes and further north of that point. He had no indication that the reef claws and shoals reached another thirty minutes, or thirty-five miles, further south. Willem de Vlamingh, who was responsible for the major Southland portion of the standard VOC map in Steyns' possession, had passed inside the islands between the shoals and the mainland on his 1697 voyage through the thirty-mile wide passage named Geelvinck Channel after his flag-ship, and had not sighted the Abrolhos. He was no help on the matter. . . .

The lower Abrolhos islands lay right across their bow, reefs awash, and spread like a net to catch the ship.

At night, the low white islands and surf-fringed reefs became wraiths. Ghosts on the sea, lost in the reflection of the waters or the gleam of the moon. Ship-wreck islands.

The *Zeewyk* was headed straight for the southernmost group, fringed and fenced by a western reef rising up out of deep water and extending for nearly fourteen miles in length. A huge surf, the full weight of the swell of the Indian Ocean, beat heavily upon it. She would come upon it at the most dangerous time of all. Change of light. The first two hours after sundown, when the lookout's eyes are not fully adjusted to the night.

They estimated that they sailed thirty miles that day. The last the *Zeewyk* would ever sail. At sunset the men ate their meal as usual; soup, saltfish, peas, and ship's biscuit, with a grog ration. There were prayers, and the usual sick parade, and the skipper and officers went down into the great cabin for their evening meal.

Van der Graeff wrote his daily entry in the familiar laborious, but well-scripted hand, with the elaborate scrolls and loops fashionable at that time, the quill dipping regularly in the lead inkwell, and scratching on a fresh page of the log: "At sunset the third mate Joris Forkson as well as a good seaman named Jan de Balande, who had been abroad before, were sent up to the mast top to keep a sharp lookout, but they could see nothing." The gathering darkness, with the sun setting behind them, made an indiscernible mark of the north-eastern horizon.

"At dusk therefore, we were running under small sail, foresail and both top-sails double-reefed, when about 7.30 in the evening the skipper Jan Steyns and the under-merchant Jan Nebbens, came up on to the quarterdeck from the master's cabin."

Steyns' glance swept the deck perfunctorily. His normal check. Suddenly he stiffened as though he could not believe what his eyes saw beyond the bowsprit.

He grabbed the arm of the officer of the watch with a grip that made the man wince, and ". . . Asked the third mate Joris Forkson who had the watch, 'What is that? . . . What is it that can be seen ahead?' Answering himself at the same moment. 'My God! It is surf! Lay your helm to starboard!'"

He shouted at the top of his voice for the second and third mates, Pieter Langeweg and Adriaen van der Graeff, who were laying out the course in the second mate's cabin. The merchant scurried straddle-legged to warn them, his self-importance frozen by the chill of fear. But they had already heard the urgency in Steyns' shout, and flinging their rulers and dividers aside ran to the stairways, jumping down them into the waist and heading for the sheets and braces.

"But before the foresails could be braced to the wind the ship crashed with a great shock into the reef on her starboard side, and turning her head into the wind around the SW knocked her rudder out of the helm port."

There was a moment's awful silence. Then a cry of shock and horror swelled from the throats of the men on deck and below and was torn away on the wind. God have Mercy! Their ship was wrecked!

In a minute their secure orderly floating world, with the routines which were now second nature after the long months at sea, became chaos. Sails thrashed overhead, flapping and banging out of control. Blocks and braces were whistling lethally loose through the air above the deck. The poor *Zeewyk* canted over on her broken side, shuddering with her injury. The sudden cessation of forward movement was the most terrifying thing after the accustomed dip and roll of her seaward passage.

Over all was a new and ominous sound—the terrible thunder and percussion of the surf, assaulting their eardrums like a physical force so that they could not hear one another's shouts and cries and could only see the mouths flapping grotesquely, below terror-widened eyes.

The surf! It roared in the darkness around her, flailing her with white sheets of spray. Pounding her hull with the hammering of hundreds of tons of green water. Great waves roaring on again to break somewhere out in the darkness ahead of them.

Where were they? On a reef-edge, a rock, or a sandbank? Stranded on the beach of the mainland, or perched on a mid-ocean spire of reef? Eyes strained in the darkness, but there was nothing to see except the breaking waves around them, and blackness beyond. No way of telling whether land lay 100 yards or 100 miles away.

The officers pushed roughly past the babbling panic-stricken soldiers and seamen. They knew what had to be done.

"At the skipper's orders I, Adriaen van der Graeff, second mate, made my way to the steerage and found there to be 8 ft. of water in the ship. Where-upon our mainmast fell overboard. . . ."

It came crashing down like a felled giant out of the black sky. 150 feet long, and many tons of lethal weight of mast, sails, and cordage, smashing, splashing into the white boil of surf alongside. . . .

"We then decided to cut our fore and mizzen masts, and found our ship to be lying in 10 to 11 ft. of water. So that we prayed to the Almighty for a propitious outcome. Terrible waves washed over us constantly while we attempted to cut away the spare timbers and spars lashed on deck. A seaman named Yuriaen Roelofsen was washed overboard together with the foremast and bowsprit, and we looked

90

at one another sorrowfully and prayed for surcease from the terrible punishment the Lord was sending us."

The ship was lost. She drew eighteen feet, under sail, and her momentum and the huge surf had carried her up the bank of reef into ten feet of water. She was breached and filled, and could never float again. They could only hope to save themselves, and then only if she could last out the night without pounding to pieces. They prayed she would hold together, and that in the morning, by God's Mercy, they might see some land nearby. To this end they cut away all their deck gear against the dread possibility of her being rolled over by the waves, and trapping them like rats in a cage.

Of course they had questioned the lookout, "whose name was Pieter de Klerk van Apel. . . . He confessed at once that he had seen the surf for at least half-an-hour; but had imagined that it was caused by the light of the sky or moon."

He was lucky they did not kill him; the traditional fate of errant lookouts in those days. But the common hands, the rough sailors and soldiers who were ready enough at most times with fists or knives, were too frightened and cowed by imminent peril to think of revenge at this time. The thought would occur later.

One other man was also alone, as the surf thundered wild and triumphant around the wreck of his fine ship. He was Jan Steyns, who had wanted to see the Southland, and had brought ruin upon them.

"Skipper what have you done, that you have run this noose around our necks?" cried Pelsaert of his skipper Ariaen Jacobsz on the poop of the wrecked *Batavia* in 1629.

There must have been similar reproach and accusation aboard the *Zeewyk*, on that dreadful night in June, 1727. Perhaps it would have been better if he had made no excuse at all, but he was human. "We have heard since from the Skipper he was to have called a ship's council at 8 o'clock in the evening to decide changing the course to NW . . ."

The night was a limbo of blackness with the phosphorous boil of the surf all around them. Where were the ship-follower sharks? Swimming close under the arching, crashing swells, waiting for the ship to break up. They shuddered at the thought.

Long before dawn they were peering into the greying east, for a mainland, or an island, or (Pray God!) even a rock, dry above the waves, on which they might save themselves if the ship broke up.

"We could see nothing but the surf which broke over the ship in an awful way." Van der Graeff, still quilling his entries by candlelight, in the midst of outer darkness and inward despair, found his routine task was a straw of sanity to clutch at in a world turned mad.

A cry of joy as the light came on the water. "At daybreak we observe 10 to 12 islands; the largest and northernmost bore to the SE of us at about $1\frac{1}{2}$ miles. As far as we could see we assume these to be the islands of Fredrik Houtman. We also observe that our top-hamper of spars and spare timbers chained together is aground on a flat reef about 300 ft. astern, and extending athwart behind the wreck as far as we can see. We inspect the hold and find that our water casks are brackish because of the salt water washing over them. But the wreck is lying over on her starboard side, and the bread store to starboard is still dry on top. Wherefore we took as much bread as we could and we look to the Almighty that He will be merciful enough to us to grant a falling of the surf so that we can lower the yawl and the longboat and reach one of the islands and pray there to God for further succour."

Another night in the blackness, but much of the terror gone because the surf was dropping, and the islands out ahead of them now offered some hope of life.

The common hands, courage revived, broke open the cargo of wine and spirits. "What better way to die than drunk?" they cried with swaggering braggadocio. A gin-courage lacking the night before, when they whimpered with death close at their elbows.

Wednesday, 11 June 1727: "It was decided to lower the yawl, and then to see whether the longboat could be lowered and taken across the reef. But while lowering the yawl the foremost of the lowering sheers broke, so that the yawl fell bow-first into the sea, through which a seaman named Jan Mus perished. The other two who were with him got back on board safely, with God's help, and the yawl floated full of water."

Long faces and glum looks. Somewhere under the water, sparkling green in the sunshine, over the coral clumps and the seaweed meadows of the bottom of the sea drifted Jan Mus, eyes closed as though sleeping.

Soon enough, the sharks would begin circling this strange and unfamiliar object. The quick grey whaler sharks of the Abrolhos, low-bellied and pugnacious. In the background, perhaps, the brown shadow of a tiger shark. Usually one senior tiger, by right of conquest, patrols a reef. An old shark, long as a whale-boat, with a striped rough hide, a square head as wide across as a table, and a dark wary eye full of cunning and malice. *Tiger, tiger, burning bright. . . .*

The sharks could sense death and fear from a long way off. There would have been many vibrations of fear coming from the wooden hull of the *Zeewyk* on the reef.

Better not to think about them. Understeersman van der Graeff was penning his journal again. "The yawl remained awash and afloat astern of the ship. We could not haul her alongside through the heavy surf, so that we had to let her run out on a line behind the break around the ship and further hope for the favour of the Lord, for all human effort seems vain. . . ."

They were sick at heart. Discouraged. In the afternoon, a seaman called Jan Croon fell overboard and drowned.

9
A Precious
Oath to God

IT WAS FORTUNATE FOR THE MEN TRAPPED IN THE MASTLESS
hull of the wreck on the reef that they did not know their
real danger.

This lay in the crucial time of the year at which they had
run onto the Abrolhos. June: the month of storms.

The southern autumn was just over. The blue skies and
millpond calms of late summer had gone. The sea was a
darker murky colour. Clouds in the sky, and a long heavy
swell rolling from the south foretold the coming winter. The
days were shorter and colder.

Soon, in a normal year, there would come the rumbling,
growling, break of the season. The winter monsoon,
heralded by a bank of black clouds piling on the north-
western horizon, and followed by gales of wind and rain
lasting from a day to a week.

Consistently in June and July, intermittently in August,
the north-west gales lash the thirteen-mile reef which protects
the southern group of Abrolhos Islands like a bastion. The
wind gradually veers through west to south with clearing

showers, and then swings back around the compass through the east to nor'west, with repeated rain and wind.

Modern crayfishermen, who fish the reef in March, April, and May, know from bitter experience that if they do not get their crayfish pots out of the reef waters by June they stand to lose them altogether in the storms which will follow. The pots smashed, splintered, and broken open by giant waves; ropes and floats chafed off and washed away, to drift back up on beaches months later with festoons of gooseneck barnacles telling of long travels on the open ocean.

Sometimes the winds reach cyclone force, and gusts of sixty to eighty miles per hour in a strong nor'westerly blow are common enough. On the big reef the waves break thirty to forty feet high, with spray and spume flung high in the air so that they can be seen from many miles away. The reef shallows become a maelstrom of turbulent seething foam, buried deep in the high tide that comes with a gale.

By ordinary standards the reef is unapproachable in mid-winter. The surf runs consistently high and long, until the spring comes with new sunshine in September.

The *Zeewyk* had stranded just when the break in the season might be expected, bringing the first immense storm to overwhelm and bury her in foam and fury. And whereas in March her crew could have paddled easily to the reef on rafts or in their boats, from June onwards they could expect rows of hungry breakers day after day. Luckily for their already shaken morale, they did not know this.

They knew the Land of Eendracht was one of those crazy upside-down places where the hot breath of summer falls at Christmas, when there should be snow and snug fires. But there was little information on Southland local weather conditions, and there had been no reason for any of the *Zeewyk*'s officers to study what there was. They had not intended to be there.

Now, trapped on the reef, their main thought was of how to reach the islands which lay on the other side, in the protection of the coral barrier.

At first they did not wish to risk the longboat, for she was their one means of sending news of their plight to Batavia.

Though she could only take a few of the best seamen, the hopes of rescue of the rest of them depended on her.

On Thursday, 12 June, five days after the wreck, they built a flat-bottomed scow of a kind familiar on the shallow waters of the Netherlands, but it was too rough to launch it. On Friday the thirteenth, they allowed the volunteer seaman Leendert Jansen, seemingly unworried by the ominous day and date, to try to swim with a line to the reef to tie to the stranded top-hamper so that the scow could be pulled along towards it. The exuberant current sucked him under in the backwash from the reef. "We were compelled to haul him aboard again and found him all but lifeless. However we succeeded through God's help in making him vomit, through which he came-to again. Then we decided to make a catamaran such as is used on the coasts of Coromandel and Malabar."

Another night fell, with the surf rising again. "We once more put ourselves in the hands of the Almighty, for he who calls on the help of mortals is always disillusioned, but He has never failed us."

Next day, the attention of van der Graeff and the officers was unpleasantly directed from scows and catamarans to a new problem. "We have found that several God-forsaken wretches and malignants in the wreck are breaking up everything and are getting intoxicated like animals between decks. It was decided this forenoon by the whole Council, not only of superior and petty officers, but also by seamen and soldiers that we would all swear a precious oath to God to be loyal to one another and faithful to the Company, and to punish together, be it even with death, all evil-doers and malignants. Those who wrote the oath are:

Officers abaft the mast:

Jan Steyns	master
Jan Nebbens	undermerchant
Pieter Langeweg	1st officer
Adriaen v.d. Graeff	2nd mate
Joris Forkson	3rd mate
Leendert Vloo	chaplain

Jan d'Bood	chief surgeon
Pieter Vekele	OC soldiers

Petty Officers:

Christiaen Radis	boatswain
David Gossiers	boatswain's mate (rigging)
Christiaen Melo	gunner
Coenraed Snoeck	chief carpenter
Andries Cornelissen	2nd carpenter
Anthony Hybeeck	3rd carpenter
Jan de Waeter	quartermaster
Frans Leban	quartermaster
Abraham v.d. Eede	quartermaster
Dirck Jansen	quartermaster
Melgyaer de Yonghe	2nd surgeon
Evert Blonke Byle	steward
Jan Vroom	3rd surgeon
Christiaen Uluyck	military corporal
Jacob Smit	private 1st class
Iacob v. Couwenberghe	chief cooper
Giliaen Pietersen	under cooper
Jan Pietersen	boatswain's mate
Jacob Stelle	boatswain's mate
Albert Hendrickse	gunner's mate
Dirck Slopman	chief sailmaker

Seamen:

Hendrick Aelberghe	Jan Meyer
Sweris Pieterse	Jan Clasen Bras
Sweris Dirckse	Jacob Clasen
Jan Ried	Jan v. Schelle
Samuel Lourense	Yuriaen Symansen
Dirck Theunisse	Jacob v.d. Spul
Dirck Pieterse	Jan d'Bruan
Emanuel Vyant	Maerten Dircksen
Elyas v. Nirens	Robbert v.d. Zwaen
Hendrick Ego	Anthony Caspersen
Hendrick Armanse	Dirck v.d. Bosch
Jacob Ubregt	Fredryck Cason
Jan Sybrantse	Gerrit v.d. Vlught
Jan de Balande	Hendrick Looff
Jan Molyn	Jacob Pietersen
Jacob Smit	Lourens Jansen
Maerten v. Coutine	Pieter v. Clerck

Pieter Francke
Willem d'Jonghe
Dirck Dircksen
Jan Thieleman
Isaeck Orleyn
Pieter Engelsen (boy)
Jan Clip (boy)
Andries Spoor (boy)
Cornelis Sury (boy)

Rynier de Graeff, cook
David Gremont (boy)
Govert Govertsen (boy)
Balten Gilles (boy)
Yuriaen Willemse (boy)
Andries Holleman (boy)
Pieter Groenwint (boy)
Pieter Ackerman (boy)

Seamen from the Cape:
Pieter d'Bruyn
Hendrick d'Bruyn
Jan Ceblans

Jan Baender
Gerrit Bick
Willem Bosch

Military:
Yuriaen Harier
Coenraed Stoffesel
Claes Jansen
Frans Wigman
Cornelis Celderjongen
Ambrosyns v. Dabele
Barent Meesa
Dominicus Bybeeck
Fred. Waldraed
    (drummer)
Hendrick Brule
Jan v. Campe-corporal
Joost Jansen
Jan d'Graeff
Jan d'Can
Jan Hyblom
Maerten v. Ekeren
Matthys Saclens
Pieter Hoghe
Theodorus Wigman

Hendrick Meyer
Christiaen Holst
Frans Egeman
Sander Sandersen
Anthony Pylaty
Andries Wynkel
Dirck v.d. Merhorst
Frans v.d. Graght
Giliaen d'Booey
Hendrick v.d. Stelle
Jan Baptist Parans
Yodocus Arrou
Jan Stroowinder
Euronemus Yostatyns
Lourens Fonteyne
Marcellis Backer
Nicolaes Muers
Pieter Luening
Thomas Cruyck

The signatures and the threat of death sobered the riotous revellers—for the moment.

On the afternoon of the fourteenth a new volunteer, Jan de Bruyn, offered to try to reach the reef on two casks lashed together, trailing a lead line painter—thin and strong so as not to offer resistance to the current. "But when it had been lowered aft he could not get on to it." Or perhaps he thought of Leendert Jansen and changed his mind.

"Another seaman, Sander Sanderson, reached the reef on it after much trouble in making his way there. When he got there he found that the leadline had been cut to pieces on the foul coral so that it was no use any longer and we had to let him spend the night on the top-hamper without being able to offer him any help."

Perched wet and cold, like a cormorant, on the heap of chained spars and spare timbers, Sanderson sat shivering until daylight, wide-eyed with fear, watching the crabs, and crayfish, and octopuses crawl over the reef. Swirls and bubbles of phosphorus in the darkness of small sharks and rays; slimy things with slimy legs oozing over the corals past his man-made island. A living nightmare . . .

Next day, 15 June, there were three more volunteers. Jacob Stelle the boatswain's mate, and two seamen, Pieter Franke and Dirk Theunisse. . . . "Who also reached the reef with great difficulty." Again the line broke on the snaring corals.

"We could not run out any more line to them, which was a great pity because all hope of saving them seemed to be exhausted." However at sunset they managed to float a barrel of victuals to them. "So that God granting they might get it and so remain alive, which happened through the blessing of the most High."

Then another night of horror on the reef with the phosphorus swirls and movement of formless things.

Things were scarcely better on the ship. "Once more at night we were in great fear because of the huge and heavy seas which washed over our wreck incessantly. At daybreak we look astern and see that the four men who went out yesterday are still alive through God's protection. They

99

called out to us in great distress, but we could not give them any help since sea and surf washed over us so strongly that it seemed as if the wreck would be dashed to pieces at any moment. We also observe that the wreck is turning over more and more on her beam and fear that it will be thrust over, the sea looked so fearsome."

The wind swung to the north-west—the danger quarter—and during the night the whole wreck was lifted up and swung around in a starboard direction by the waves.

"We therefore fell at the feet of the Lord and prayed together for His help and succour, whereupon we perceived clearly that the Omnipotent hears our prayer for shortly afterwards the wind veered to the S, its force and the surf decreasing, and before dawn it even swung SSE with topsail force."

This was what they needed. An easterly wind, blowing back over the top of the reef to flatten the surf. A wind common in summer, but rare in June.

They were badly shaken by the night's experience, and the spray-drenched men on the reef, clinging like crabs to the top-hamper, were more dead than alive.

It was now the seventh day after the wreck, and they were becoming desperate to get off the ship. They decided to risk the longboat, "Since we had previously prepared her with the whole crew. For this purpose we have lowered three spars on top of each other behind the fo'castle, as well as fitting the main top-yard, the square yard, and the main top-gallant yard with suitable gin tackle. We also made buffers of half-anchor stocks under the boat's belly as skids for the reef. At about 2 in the afternoon we swung her overboard with God's help, and she lay very conveniently alongside."

Though she was a big craft by small-boat standards, between twenty-five and thirty feet long, and beamy in proportion, "We could get no more than 12 men into her, and these reached the reef successfully."

But when they tried to pull in the cable she had been towing to steady her through the surf, to take off another load of men, it also fouled in the corals.

100

So they lowered the scow overboard with thirteen men in her, to pull themselves along the cable to the reef. It was an unlucky number. "She was flooded by the surf, and got fouled at the cable, which they had to cut through in the scow. Consequently, eight men drowned and lost their lives, the other five saving themselves by swimming to the reef. The scow was also tossed on the reef."

There were then twenty-two men on the reef with the longboat and top-hamper, and the righted scow of ill-fortune. Walking about on the rocks they made a curious and ominous discovery—one which must have made their hearts sink more than a little. They were not the first ship there.

"They found a filled hand-grenade, also old rope and ship's skin these belonging to a ship or ships which the same fate had struck here . . ." The ghosts sat with them on the reef that night.

17 June, and the watchers on the ship saw the longboat row to the nearest island behind the reef, an island they were all to come to know well in the months that followed. The boat remained there three hours and pitched a tent, returning to the reef "Where they arrived about noon and indicated to us by signal that they had found fresh water. This gladdened us extraordinarily since in the wreck seawater was washing over our water barrels and no more was to be had."

On the eighteenth the sun rose on a beautiful morning, calm and still, and the main exodus from the wreck began. They had dismantled the wooden sun-shelter awning from the quarterdeck (contemptuously called a "cow-bridge" by English seamen, but very useful in the present situation) and made rafts from it.

During the afternoon twenty-one men crossed to the reef on the rafts, and it was so calm the second sailmaker even swam across. Victuals were floated across the 100-yard gap in barrels and picked up by men wading on top of the reef.

Next day the fine weather held. Jan Steyns, Jan Nebbens, and four other men crossed to the reef. Van der Graeff was left in charge on the wreck with seventy-one men, including Joris Forkson the third mate and Christiaen Radis the boatswain. Van der Graeff's first command was a broken ship, but he set his men vigorously to work making more rafts and throwing victuals overboard in barrels, building up a supply for their expected sojourn on the island.

That evening, he settled down to record the day's activities in unaccustomed luxury, but had time to write only a few words. "At 7 o'clock I, Adriaen van der Graeff was writing up the journal in the skipper's cabin . . ." Then there was a disturbance. "The boatswain's mate Jacob Jan Pietersen with three or four other men dragged in Jacob Pietersen, ordinary seaman. All hands came running up stating he was making a great uproar 'tween decks, breaking open cupboards and seachests and threatening people who spoke to him." They found five sharpened knives on the drunken sailor, and flung him in irons.

Their good weather had almost run its course. On Thursday, 19 June 1727, the wind began to shift back to the north-west, and the surf to rise again. Their time was running out and with a sense of urgency, van der Graeff had a stack of victual barrels piled on deck, and rafts made ready to take off all hands. But at two p.m., with a freshening wind and the surf booming ominously, a crisis arose.

The common hands refused to leave the wreck, either from a fear of the rising surf, or a reluctance to end their joyful forays into the *Zeewyk*'s cargo of liquor.

"We could not move the hardened hearts of many of the crew since about half those malignants would not help us, saying that they wanted to remain on the wreck. We found ourselves compelled to launch our own rafts. Therefore we threw over the victuals which we had barrelled, lowered away our rafts, and so floated to the reef at God's Mercy, which we reached with the help of the Almighty without any of us being lost. Among whom was I, Adriaen van der Graeff, second mate; Joris Forkson, third mate; and Christiaen Radis, boatswain, and some more men.

"Bringing with me also, barrelled in a cask and previously thrown overboard, the ship's papers which came to the reef and then to the island in a dry condition and which I have handed over to the skipper Jan Steyns."

They gathered up the half-filled victual barrels bobbing about in the reef-top shallows, and with the tide rising at one o'clock in the morning set off for the island at first light in the longboat. Friday the twentieth was a day of thunderstorms and drenching showers, and trips back and forth to the reef for men and victuals. At last all the willing hands were on the island. A morning muster call at eight a.m. on Saturday, 31 June 1727, showed that there were ninety-six men on the beach, including all the officers and petty officers. They had a considerable quantity of rations of meat, bacon, butter, wine, bread and brandy; two boats (the longboat and the scow) and the makeshift rafts. The yawl, to their great regret, had broken its cable behind the ship while full of water, and drifted away.

But for the moment they were safe. There was water on the island. They had the stout seaworthy longboat, with charts and navigation instruments. Things were much better than they might have been, or than they had appeared to be twelve days before.

As was proper the assembled company thanked God on their knees for their deliverance, while the island cormorants and terns, and perhaps a shaggy seal or two, watched and wondered.

Deliverance to what, was to be the question.

10
Gritty Pancakes
on the Sea

THE *Zeewyk* MEN, AND JAN STEYNS IN PARTICULAR, MUST HAVE often thought about the part played by luck in the wrecking of their ship.

They could have been excused a certain bitterness about the Fate that set them on their reef.

If the *Zeewyk* had sailed a bare two miles farther north, after all the thousands of miles she had sailed from Africa, she would have missed the reef and sailed unharmed through the Albrolhos during the night.

Or if the ship had been two hours faster on her eight month voyage, the watch would have seen the surf in daylight.

Even as things were, if silly Pieter de Klerk van Apel who thought he saw moonbeams had asked someone with more experience about the white flashes he saw ahead, they could have still saved the vessel.

The lives and fortunes of men—our own as well as those of the *Zeewyk* crew so long ago—hang on such slender threads.

But if they were unlucky to be wrecked, the *Zeewyk*'s crew at least were fortunate in the islands where they came ashore.

Gun Island, where they landed, was one of the few of all the hundreds of cays in the Abrolhos where they could quickly find fresh water, and this only at the time of year in which they arrived. Without the first rains of the winter trapped in natural rock cisterns and hollows, they might well have died in the first few days and left their bones to whiten in the sun, and Van der Graeff's journal, with its careful entries, to blow in the sand of a rotted tent, with the dead men all around . . .

The islands are completely different from the coast of the mainland, about forty miles away. Gun Island is a quarter-mile-long rock platform with narrow beaches and surrounded by bare, sea-swept coral flats.

Other islands are simply sandspits, or wave-piled heaps of loose coral flags which twist underfoot and make walking on them an ankle-turning hazard.

Vegetation is generally sparse. Salt bushes, struggling for a foothold, bind the sand together, and push roots into rock fissures. On some islands there are clusters of swaying olive-leafed mangroves with finger-like roots poking out of the sand. Fish and crabs peer from among the shadows.

Most of the mangroves are thin and spindly, but on the large island of the southern group, a skinny six-mile spine which is only a few yards across in places, they have bloomed to magnificence by the lagoons. Stately trees, thicker than a man's chest, and though low in silhouette with branches reaching out from twenty to thirty feet. The ground below them is whitened with the droppings of tens of thousands of screeching Noddy terns, which nest in their protective foliage.

There are three main groups of islands in the Abrolhos Archipelago, with twenty-six fathom channels running between them. They are the Wallabi group, the Easter group, and the Pelsaert group. Each is a separate coral atoll like those of the northern Barrier Reef, the Cocos Islands in the Indian Ocean, and Bikini Atoll in the Pacific. They cover about fifty miles of ocean from south to north with their patterns of reefs. The closest points to the mainland are thirty-one miles at the south end islands, where the *Zeewyk* was wrecked. North Island, the extreme northern point, lies a little further out to sea.

The biggest islands lie to the north. They are East and West Wallabi, the islands of Weibbe Hayes, which stand as much as sixty feet above sea level and are two and three miles long. They are named after little hopping rock wallabies, descendants of those which kept Hayes and the *Batavia* loyalists alive in 1629.

The *Zeewyk* men did not sight Pelsaert's islands, and only had a fleeting glimpse of the central atoll, later to be called the Easter Group.

The Albrolhos atolls on whose outer rim they found themselves are formed by coral reefs on the edge of the Australian Continental Shelf. The banks of polyp-created lime deposits, growing up from twenty-five fathoms, are the southernmost large coral formations in the world.

None of the islands in the south, where the *Zeewyk* men found themselves, are more than fifteen feet above sea level. Most are much less. They have changed very little in two-and-a-half centuries, and today look exactly as the Dutch castaways must have seen them.

From a distance, they appear as half-tide banks, as Pelsaert remarked in his 1629 journal. Gritty pancakes flat on the sea, smelling strongly of ammonia from sea-bird droppings, and looking so deceptively fragile that you would hardly expect them to resist a winter storm.

Two hundred miles north of the Abrolhos, where Dirk Hartog first saw the Western Australian coast, the scene is different. The sea and the land lie in titanic conflict. Giant swells from the Indian Ocean explode in mountains and sheets of salt spray, flailing hundreds of feet up sheer red cliffs. On a rough day at the height of Womeranji, just south of Shark Bay, spume falls in a drizzle-like rain over the crest, 1,000 feet above the sea. The same warrior waves might be expected to wash contemptuously over the Abrolhos cays, gobbling the few hard-won acres like a shark. But the reefs are a marvellous protection.

The wave crests, after thousands of miles of open ocean, arch hungrily from the deep water as though to strike and swallow the presumptuous scraps of dry land. The tops curl and run with a hissing roar as the attack is launched. Then the reef adroitly catches the wall of water at the knees. The wave topples and collapses in a frustrated spout of spume; momentum killed, strength stolen away. A weak wall of bubbles and backwash laps against the island, and then the next wave is arching and puffing its chest, riding for its fall in turn.

The Dutch sailors probably found the banks and shallows of the Abrolhos less strange than modern Australians coming from the mainland, because they hailed from a country of low-lying islands; the Netherlands, or "Low Countries."

Especially the men from Zeeland, which in English means "Sea-Land." This was a territory of linked channels, tide-flats, and islands. North Sea fishing had made them experts in handling small boats in surf and shallows. Their practical sailing experience, and familiarity with primitive but easily-improvised navigation methods, had probably equipped them better to handle the Robinson Crusoe situation in which they found themselves than a modern ship's crew stranded in the same circumstances.

In years before the *Zeewyk* wreck, other Dutchmen had proved themselves tough and resourceful castaways on the South Land coast. They were hard men to kill, but Indiamen crews had died nevertheless. Perished miserably, in fact, and though the *Zeewyk* men had a temporary respite from the hard realities of survival, it did not diminish their ultimate danger.

The chief problem was their number. Ninety-six hungry bellies and thirsty throats over-taxing their resources of food and water, besides the twenty or thirty men on the wreck who might be expected to come ashore as soon as the novelty of an endless party in the *Zeewyk*'s liquor cargo had worn off. Nursing their brandy heads. Glowering with reddened eyes. Demanding food and drink in the uncouth tones of the Common Hands, with a new note of peremptory insolence. Allying themselves with their lower deck cronies already ashore, who were likely to be in dangerous mood.

On board ship they could be whipped, flogged, even hanged, for breaches of discipline and insubordination. There was a whole machinery for keeping them cowed and servile. But a shipwreck changed all that. The officers had lost the men's respect by wrecking the ship. They were to blame. As castaways they were all equal, and if the officers did not already realize this unpalatable fact it was shortly to be brought forcibly home to them.

With limited food and water, and a large group of men in ugly mood—who would regard efforts at survival iron-rationing as simply attempts to deprive them of their rights—the *Zeewyk* officers were under severe test. To save the ship's company, to escape from the trap into which they had fallen, they had to have a rescue ship—either built by themselves, which seemed out of the question at the moment, or summoned from Batavia by a crew of picked men who would sail there in the longboat. They would have to cross 1,700 miles of open sea, with storms, hunger, and dreadful thirst on the way. Four of the fourteen of Abraham Leeman's boat crew had survived in 1656. Could the *Zeewyk*'s longboat be relied upon to reach Batavia?

For the first few days they had been largely occupied in erecting their tents (which they at first unwisely faced to the westerly weather quarter), organizing their messes, and burying men for whom the transition from ship to shore had been suddenly too much. In four days Jan van Zelm, a corporal shipped at the Cape of Good Hope; Frans Egeman, soldier; and Anthony Casperson, seaman, all died, and were buried in the southerly sandhills of the island.

Their surviving comrades were overjoyed to find large hair seals (*Neophoca cinera*) on the beaches. Being rather stupid and never having seen men before, the inoffensive creatures were easily killed. "But it is to be expected that they will become timid, from which God protect us" . . . (But not the seals) . . . "There is also a kind of scrub here in which the island abounds which we can use for fuel so that we can roast seal meat over a fire."

On 26 June, the carpenter began making a mast for the longboat. "We planning to voyage to Batavia in her with the blessing of the Most High. I am hoping for the rescue of all of us," wrote van der Graeff in a new mood of optimism.

The longboat sailed to the reef daily. Its crew picked up timber for the camp and for building small boats, stores thrown over by the men on the wreck, and even men themselves; those who were regretting their decision to stay on board, and were coming in to the reef on rafts and casks in twos and threes. Sometimes, due to low tides—the once-daily tides of the Abrolhos had the Dutchmen confused and perplexed at first—they had to wait on the reef several days before being taken off.

There was one curious incident which is worth relating because of the aftermath, months later. A boy named Pieter Engels, who had gone to the reef in the longboat, refused to go back to the island, but remained sitting on the top-hamper on the reef. The weather was rough and the boat was over-crowded, but there was no danger on the short passage to the island, in sheltered water inside the reef. Why should he refuse to go, to choose to stay in cold and peril, unless he had quarrelled with someone, or they had bullied him? He must have been desperately afraid or unhappy, because he stayed on the reef for seven days, in stormy, squally weather. The men on the ship floated victuals to him.

The crisis with the Common Hands came to a head on 1 July. "At 7 o'clock in the morning all the Common Hands and the petty officers, most of whom were drunk, walked into our (the officers) tent with a great deal of clamour and confusion and argument and counter-argument. All shouting at the same time. Telling the skipper that they wanted the longboat to sail to Batavia and that they wished to appoint as her chief the first mate Pieter Langeweg and no-one else, and 10 of the best seamen with him." Van der Graeff's dream of going himself was dashed. The officers had to swallow their pride or face the threat of a general mutiny.

"They will hear of no further counsel saying that . . . they have collected some good seamen whom they deem to be capable of handling a longboat and have appointed 10 of them according to lots drawn, to sail in the boat. These being: Jan Ried, Pieter d'Bruyn, Juriaen Symonsen, Jan van Sorelle, Hendrik Aelberghan, Emanuel Vyant, Lennert Jansen, Sander Sandersen, Christiaen Holst, Dirk Pietersen."

These included all the men who had distinguished themselves as volunteers in the difficult days of getting to the reef from the ship. The best men were among them. A week later, and again by general request, the name Jacob Ubertsen was added to the list.

The next few days were spent getting the longboat ready, building a deck, and fitting sails. She sailed on Thursday, 10 July, with fine, calm conditions, the wind east and east-south-east. "At sunset the longboat set sail for Batavia, may God guide her." The crew was the one selected by the new masters, the Common Hands, including the last-minute addition Ubertsen. But if van der Graeff wished himself aboard, as her sail disappeared in the open sea, he would ultimately be thankful he stayed behind. The boat and the crew were never seen again.

With the longboat's departure, the lives of the officers became almost intolerable. The soldiers and seamen had them at their beck and call, and thoroughly enjoyed playing the tune to which the discomfited puppets danced. Van der Graeff's July entries are a mixture of petulance, outrage, and private despair.

10 July: ". . . This afternoon we were ordered by the Common Hands to distribute among the crew two barrels of wine which were in our tent . . ."

11 July: "Shortly after midday all the rabble, as well as the petty officers, came up and ordered us to hand out a barrel of wine to be distributed in equal portions which we did, giving ourselves an equal share to theirs. There were also 5 Edam cheeses which we handed out too, as well as some tobacco and six kegs of salted salmon and sturgeon which we also shared out in equal portions. . . ."

The breakdown in discipline had its inevitable effects.

"During the distribution of the wine a great clamour arose among the Common Hands. Four men began to brandish

110

knives, striking one another and throwing some of the wine into their fires, and doing the same with their food which is badly needed here. We were apprised this evening when about 7 o'clock the boatswain and gunner entered our tent, very dismayed, telling us everything which I have related here. That is to say that the chief cooper, the drummer, and a soldier are causing a great uproar on the island striking everyone they encounter, uttering great curses and oathes, and throwing people's rations into the fire saying 'Let the dog burn!' . . ."

This was too much. On board ship a man could traditionally be flogged for spilling more food or drink than a hand or foot could cover. This food was being thrown away when they might face starvation later. The Council met hurriedly, and the men, Jacob van Couwenberghe the chief cooper, Fredrik Waldraed the drummer, and Hendrik van Stelle the soldier, were seized and put under guard with their hands and feet tied. A little while later there was a complaint that the wine had also turned the head of the boatswain's mate, David Gossier. "Having an argument he drew his knife and wanted to attack his accuser, the truthfulness of which statement was corroborated by seven or eight people." Gossier was grabbed, trussed, and laid with the other three glowering trouble-makers.

It was a delicate situation. Badly handled it might easily provoke a mutiny among the muttering Common Hands. On the other hand if the recalcitrants were allowed to go unpunished there would soon be anarchy on the island and all restraint would be gone.

The council of officers diplomatically invited the Common Hands to join them in considering the matter. My Lords of the Lower Deck, enjoying the new feeling of importance, agreed to help in the judgement, and it was decided ". . . To give the miscreants a proper flogging and on a day which God might grant to be suitable weather to take them to another island situated at the SE of us about two miles. When we were there some days ago we found a good supply of firewood and many seals on which they can feed. Inasmuch as we fear that staying here they will persist in their re-

111

calcitrant behaviour, which they have affirmed incessantly to me and others while they lay in irons."

The sentence was carried out at 8 a.m. on Wednesday, 23 July—no reason is given for the long delay—when, "The four rebels mentioned on the 11th were punished with a flogging, and at the intercession and request of the Common Hands they were permitted to remain here on the island upon their promise to lead henceforth a Christian life."

The Common Hands had the last word after all.

While there were problems of discipline on the island there were also some troubles with the men out on the ship, many of whom now wanted nothing more than to leave it.

In fact it suited the island party quite well that there should be someone aboard the wreck, because they needed a constant supply of sail-cloth for tents and clothes, and victuals for rations. They made continual excuses for not taking them off—though to be fair the surf ran high and heavy most of the latter part of June and through July.

Messages were passed back and forth. A typical entry was on 4 July: ". . . Found on the beach a small keg with a piece of parchment nailed to the bottom on which was written 'Open This' . . . Found inside a lot of Canasse tobacco completely soaked and a parchment letter that we were to come to them in the boat to help them and then they would give us victuals. . . In the wreck they still fancy that we could reach them in the boat through the surf. Which is completely impossible. . ."

Occasionally desperate men cast themselves into the water with a keg or small raft, and were washed up on the reef. They then made for the artificial island of the top-hamper, and were picked up, sooner or later, by boat crews from the island who rowed to the reef for this purpose and to get victuals. The numbers on the wreck gradually dwindled, but the last man, Godvrinel Stroomeyer, did not come ashore until 27 October. Among the last to leave was the lookout "Moonbeam" de Klerk, who came fearfully ashore on 20 October, with a soldier named Jan Stroowinder.

As soon as they were organized in island routines, foraging parties began going out in the scows built from ship's timbers by the carpenters, to explore, hunt seals, and fish.

The islands must have been a beachcomber's paradise in those days in 1727, when they were the first men on the pristine shores. Banks of corals surrounded every island, forming lagoons and pools sometimes dropping away in submarine cliffs and canyons to 100 feet of dark blue depths within a few yards. Schools of predatory fish such as spanish mackerel, kingfish, and bonito, patrol the channels hunting smaller fish, with flocks of sea-birds wheeling excitedly overhead and diving on the scraps of the carnage.

Bright green groper and multi-coloured parrot fish, singly and in flocks, raise arrow-shaped ripples through the shallows. The tell-tale curious white feelers of rock lobsters protrude like straws from under every reef and crevice, to be dragged flopping from their refuges. They are delicious eating broiled, or grilled on the coals, when the shells turn bright red and the meat becomes white and juicy and firm.

The wings of millions of sea-birds beat the air at sunrise and sunset. Flocks pass overhead to the ocean feeding grounds, darkening the sky; shearwaters, terns, Pacific gulls, common and lesser noddies, black and pied cormorants, silver gulls, oyster catchers, the beautiful red-tailed tropic or frigate bird, boobies, mutton birds, and petrels. White breasted sea eagles and ospreys wheeling among them, like patrolling policemen.

The eggs, and—as the Dutchmen would discover—some of the birds themselves were excellent eating, but being heavy meat-eaters they were principally interested in seals. They killed the big friendly creatures in great numbers, and brought the quartered carcasses back to the island to roast over their fires. Their biggest catch was fourteen in one trip on 5 July, and there were records of other hauls that were good for the Dutchmen, but sad for the seals.

They also noted new islands dotted about, beyond the already familiar ones on their own locale. These included one which seemed to run the length of the south-eastern horizon, and which they mistakenly thought was the mainland of the Land of Eendracht.

And so they settled into their Robinson Crusoe life on the island, which up to the end of July was pleasant enough. There was plenty to eat and drink, and no shortage of luxury food from the cargo such as the salmon and sturgeon intended for the upper classes of Batavia, and fine wine and brandy never envisaged as gargle for the gullets of hairy Common Hands.

But they were closer to peril than they realized. The water on the island was beginning to run short.

11
The Beast
of Mutiny

THICK-TONGUED AND DESPERATE, THEY BEGAN SCOOPING
water with spoons from puddles left in the rock-holes by
overnight showers of rain.

The water was tainted with salt and bitter with bird
droppings, but it tasted like nectar to thirsty men. A man
can die in forty-eight hours from thirst, or even more quickly
if he is already weak from scurvy or afraid. Fear was the
worst enemy.

The killing of the weak by the strong to survive is a grue-
some but not uncommon story among castaways. The
horror of cannibalism, with men murdering comrades to
drink their blood or eat their flesh like beasts has occurred
frequently, and sadly the horror has often been unnecessary.
The fear of want, rather than the actual physical experience,
can drive men to madness before the real onset of thirst and
hunger. It is compounded by despair, loneliness, the
unbearable prospect of dying far from home, expiring like
an animal without a grave or a headstone to show that they
had lived, or the final comfort of friends and relatives.

The *Zeewyk* camp stank of fear during August. "This afternoon we learn to our great sorrow that there is no longer any fresh water to be had on the island. We beseech the Omnipotent that He may cast a merciful glance in our direction and grant us some rain to quench our natural thirst . . ."

The Common Hands began to steal each other's water and rations, and then the officers' rations also. They were frightened, and already the strongest among them were thinking what they might do if no rain fell, or if the weather prevented them getting to the wreck for the barrelled provisions.

In the eighteenth century, shipwreck was so common that no one had given the matter of survival much thought. It was God's Will, and who could provide against that?

In our own time, attitudes are rather different. In 1952, the French doctor Alain Bombard crossed the Atlantic in a rubber dinghy, taking sixty-five days for the voyage and living entirely by drinking sea-water and eating fish and plankton. He found he could drink a pint and a half of sea-water a day, and that his greatest enemy was not the ocean but himself. He had to fight the castaway's psychosis; fear and loneliness.

He wrote afterwards: "Statistics show that ninety per cent of the survivors of shipwrecks die within three days, yet it takes longer than that to (clinically) perish of hunger and thirst. When his ship goes down a man's whole universe goes with it. Because he no longer has deck under his feet his courage and reason abandon him. Even if he reaches a lifeboat he is not necessarily safe. He sits slumped, contemplating his misery, and can hardly be said to be alive. Helpless in the night, chilled by sea and wind, terrified by the solitude, by noise, and by silence, he takes less than three days to surrender his life.

"How many castaways through the ages have become stiff and sudden corpses, killed not by the sea, not by hunger or thirst but by their own terror?"

When the *Titanic* hit her iceberg in 1912, those survivors lucky enough to gain seats in a lifeboat had to wait less than three hours for rescue ships. Yet even in that short time a number of people died or went mad in the boats.

The *Zeewyk* men had survived the initial peril of the wreck, which might well have killed them all, and reached their island. They were fortunate in finding fresh water and the fact that their ship—a treasure store of provisions—did not break up as had the *Batavia* in 1629, the *Gilt Dragon* in 1656, and the *Zuytdorp* in 1712. Hendrik Raas, the Zeeland shipwright, had done his work well. The *Zeewyk*, battered by the surf, tugged by the currents, obstinately hung together. A symbol of hope and encouragement to the men on their island.

Every morning when they emerged from their tents their eyes anxiously sought her on the reef, and the faces smiled when they saw her still there. When the storms raged and the spray spouted high in the air they watched her with worry and concern. What if she should break up?

If she had, the blow to their morale by the loss of their only link with the outside world, the ship—even though she would never sail again—would probably have been mortal. It would have taken away their will to live.

In purely physical terms they could have survived with ease for the rest of their natural lives on the fish, bird, and animal life of the Abrolhos, this beachcomber's realm of abundance. But without hope a man dies quickly. And who would want to live in a fresh-air prison of stony islands and coral reefs, with gaol walls of endless ocean stretching to the horizon? Never to see the green fields of Holland, or snow, or a woman again. A woman . . . there was a thing. Many of the men were already restless for the flesh. The thoughts of some of them were turning towards each other. Sodomy. The stupid sin.

They survived their August, despite the dark perils of the mind, because the weather was kind and the storms that came were not really angry. The ship held together. But van der Graeff's journal, with constant complaints of insolence and insubordination from the Common Hands, and thefts of water and rations, shows that there was an ugly mood among the tents in the scrub-covered sand-dunes.

Fear of want, rather than any actual hardship, made the Common Hands aggressive and truculent. Mutiny was not far around the corner. After all, it was the officers who had got them in this mess. They had wrecked the ship. If anyone was to die they should perish first . . . it would be justice after all. . . .

There were times when the officers were in terror of their lives. At best they lived on the thin edge of the tolerance of the mob, maintaining a paper status only by confirming decisions which had already been made for them, and watching helplessly when their rations were contemptuously and openly stolen from them. One angry word, or hasty action in remonstrance, could have had all their throats cut, and they knew it well.

7 August. "At daybreak when we got up we saw that our seal which we received yesterday as our share of rations, and which had been hanging in front of the tent, had been stolen. We and the petty officers searched all the tents in the island but could not find it. Whereupon we looked at each other sadly because we now have little if anything to eat. . . ."

"This afternoon there happened something in the island which I deem to be very impertinent. The master, the merchant, and the predikant Lennert Vloo, had gone fishing for their amusement in the large scow, but they could not catch anything. Meantime all the hands set to work to convey all the fresh water which was in the island and kept in butts in our tent to their own tents, each man as much as he could. Since I was alone in the tent with the chief surgeon I could do nothing to stop them . . ." The beast of mutiny was stretching its claws.

8 August. "In the afternoon the skipper called all the hands together, asking them what they had in mind by taking all the water to their tents leaving us nothing. He asked whether they wanted us to perish of thirst and starvation. Whereupon they all answered unanimously that they would give us some water, each according to what he had. But we got hardly sufficient . . ."

9 August. "Rain in the late night, through which, Thank God! we obtained a barrel of water which we scooped up

with an ordinary tablespoon from the little wells in the rocks of the island during the morning . . ."

The beast was held at bay for a little longer, and on the tenth the pinch of hunger was relieved by fine weather and the fact that the scow was able to go to the reef and pick up a barrel of wine, three Edam cheeses, a keg of butter, and an anker of wet bread. These provisions were issued in an atmosphere of celebration on the eleventh. But though seals were caught on the twelfth, and more provisions were brought from the reef, van der Graeff's pen was once again scratching petulantly. "About 8 p.m. the large scow returned (from the reef) in the dark, bringing, as we saw eventually, 2 aums of wine one of which was almost empty, the other being such that together they contained almost a full aum. The skipper was warned by the chief surgeon 'the scow has come in' and going outside found three people trying to roll the fullest keg through the scrub in the island intending to conceal it from us . . . The names of the three men are Christiaen Melo, gunner, Jan de Balande, and Henrik Armanse, seamen. The officer who was in charge of the scow was the boatswain's mate (rigging) David Gossier."

On the sixteenth the scow returned from the reef and a sweet and valuable cargo was smuggled ashore by the men who had sailed her—long white clay pipes, fragrant tobacco, and a keg of mellow brandy. Somehow the reef crew got the contraband to their own tent unseen by the usually watchful eyes of their shipmates, and spent an evening of delicious and unaccustomed luxury.

There was a great howl of indignation from the Common Hands when they found how they had been cheated of their shares next day. "The Common Hands who never sail in the scow being bad seamen and soldiers raised a clamour," wrote van der Graeff unsympathetically.

Towards the end of the month the weather improved. The worst of the winter, obviously an exceptionally mild one in 1727, was over, and spring was in the air. They became optimistic about rescue. "August 18: Today we erect a flag-staff made of a lower studding-sail boom and a top-gallant mast, in order to be able to give the arranged signal to the first mate Pieter Langeweg. This being the flag of Middelburg which will henceforth fly daily."

Pieter Langeweg would not be looking for their flag. He and his crew were already dead. Whether they perished of thirst in a sun-blistered boat in the last tropic windless miles below Java, were overwhelmed by a storm at sea, or tossed on the teeth of an unknown reef, will never be known. The best and bravest men of the *Zeewyk* crew, they vanished without trace.

The men who stayed behind found more supplies of seals on the islands to the south and east. Poor seals. Gentle and inquisitive, they had no fear of the men, and fell easy victims to the thudding clubs.

The few descendants of the once great herds still have the same interest and misplaced faith in men today, despite the bloody slaughters of the centuries. They will swim around a diver, imitating his movements like playful dolphins. Their sleek whiskery heads and big brown eyes are like Labrador retriever dogs. On the beach they are slothful sun-lovers, and reluctant to move for approaching footsteps.

The Dutchmen were hungry and needed food. But later generations of Abrolhos visitors were to hunt them mercilessly for meat, blubber, bait, or just the "sport" of killing a large warm-blooded thing. Man's enthusiasm for killing other creatures for the pleasure of their deaths is his least attractive trait. It shows no sign of decreasing despite our "civilization" and increased distance from the days of the cave when we had to kill for meat to eat and for skins to clothe ourselves.

In the days of the *Zeewyk*, which were 242 years ago on our scale, but not so long in terms of history, the population of wild animals in the world was thousands of times its present dwindling level. The word extinction had not then been coined. Now it has a real meaning, and unless we gain belated wisdom it may be man's own epitaph.

On the island, where the Dutch were only worried about their own possible extinction, there occurred the phenomenon of the birds. "August 20: This evening we saw some birds flying over the island which we have never seen by day, flying close to the ground and in every direction about a man's height high, like bats do in our own country. . . ."

They were wedge-tailed shearwaters, *Puffinus pacificus*. "These birds are about the size of a young duck, black in front with a black sharp beak about 2 in. long, somewhat curved at the end, and long closed claws. At about midday the soldier named Andries Wyckel dies . . ."

So did forty-four birds, killed by sticks wielded by men of the crew's mess called "Alverloren," an ironical title meaning "Everything Lost." They plucked the black plumage off the thin little bodies and roasted them in their fires.

The birds, which spend their normal lives at sea pivoting from wing-tip to wing-tip a few feet above the waves in graceful and endless search for small squid, or floating nestled fraternally together in great rafts and roosts on the bosom of the deep, had come to shore for their annual breeding. They nest in long sandy burrows on off-shore islands, and are easily caught once they land. "This evening we (the officers) join in the hunt to catch the birds mentioned, and find them in hollows which they have in the ground and from which we pull them with our hands. We had seen an abundance of these burrows before now, but since we saw lizards run in and out of them we imagined them to be their shelters. This evening about 80 or 90 were caught, of which our mess caught 25. We also catch a seal."

The shearwaters, or "mutton-birds" (from their fatty taste) as they are known to most Australians today are better eating than might be imagined. The chicks, stuffed with fish and squid brought fluttering in by the parents, are heavier and better to eat than the adults, and form the basis of an industry on the Bass Strait Islands in which some three-quarters of a million young birds, or "squabs," are captured in the burrows, killed, salted or sold fresh, each year. Despite the fact that this has been going on more than a century, and in the early days there were no controls, the population of birds seems to be sustained. A rare example.

The Dutch knew nothing about the squabs which would have appeared later in the year after the mating and laying, and killed the adult birds with an enthusiasm which meant that—for that year at any rate—there was no successful hatching and rearing on their island.

On 27 August, the small scow beached with dramatic news. They had found the figurehead and many portions of another shipwreck on the long land to the south, which they had previously thought to be the Southland main. It was an island, about six miles long, and—best news of all— the *Zeewyk*'s yawl, last seen drifting away astern and full of water, had been washed up on its beach and was repairable.

"On the W side of the same island they found a piece of a ship, finding the figurehead under some overhanging rocks. Of which they could discern that it had been the figure of a woman. In this island there are a great many seals as well as birds. Also many kinds of fish."

It was decided that Jan Steyns should take a crew to the new island to repair the yawl and look at the wreckage, and with the end of the month came beautiful spring weather.

"Friday, August 29: In the late night, morning, and forenoon the wind E., calm, also dead calm. In the forenoon the seaman named Willem Bosch dies. In the afternoon a little breeze blew up from the sea. In the afternoon evening and early night the wind W and WSW, also SW, calm and still. This evening many birds were caught again of which 20 by us. At dusk the surgeon's mate Melgioor d'Jonge dies.

We now number 93 in the island. In the early night the large scow arrives at the island from the reef bringing a keg of butter and one of brandy which we issue at once."

The party at the long island repaired the yawl, and also found a great deal of wreckage from their own ship and the mysterious stranger. "The island from which they have fetched the yawl bears SE by E from this island extending S and N as far as they know . . . and estimated to be 4 or 5 miles long, about $\frac{1}{2}$ a mile wide in some places and in others only a pistol shot. There is nothing on it but coral and here and there a wild laurel tree, so that the master is of the opinion that it is a reef that has been thrown up. They also pulled birds from their burrows like we do here. There is also a great host of seals there, of which they brought 20."

On 10 September, with the newly repaired yawl, they got through the surf to the wreck for the first time since June, and on the fifteenth brought five of the Company's money chests to the reef. The seventeenth saw the remaining five, in calm spring weather, slung carefully over the side of the wreck and lowered into the boat for the reef. Jan Steyns, two carpenters, the boatswain's mate, the quartermaster, and five other men remained on the wreck, to carry out a more systematic unloading of the victuals than had previously been possible in the bad weather and with the unreliable hands who had stayed on board all this time.

With the landing of the money chests the officers felt a great weight of worry lift from their minds. They might have lost the ship, but they had at least saved 315,836 guilders for the Company. This was surely well done in their circumstances, despite the bedraggled condition of the wooden chests after scraping over the reef. "The Company's money chests, which look very miserable through being dragged and brought over cliffs and coral bottom, have sustained considerable damage, which could not be helped."

The treasure weighed three tons. Each box weighed about 600 pounds, and was made of wood, bound with metal bands, and with three locks. The money was in gold and silver ingots, in pieces-of-eight from Mexico, in ducatons, and "paymenten"—small change coins, such as silver schellingen (similar to an English shilling or Australian 10 cent piece), and dubbel stuivers, small silver coins the size of a sixpence.

The pieces-of-eight were the most remarkable. Heavy odd-shaped coins, they were also called Mexicanen, Pillaren, Cabo de Barra ("end-of-the-bar"), Cobs, Reales de a Ocho, Spanish Reales, Dollars, or pesos. They were a hand-made coin, and were simply discs of metal lopped from rudely cast bars of silver and stamped after being trimmed to weight with shears. Despite their rough appearance pieces-of-eight enjoyed wider circulation than any other coin in history.

Through the Spanish Manila-bound galleons sailing from Acapulco in the sixteenth, seventeenth, and eighteenth centuries, and the Dutch who traded silver coins from the

Spaniards, the pieces-of-eight became the standard unit of currency throughout Asia and indeed the world. Because of the irregular shape of the coins and their crude manufacture, counterfeiting and clipping of the Real de a Ocho—though punishable by hanging, hand-chopping or boiling alive—were very prevalent. Perhaps because of the ease of tampering with the piece-of-eight, it was very popular in China. An English visitor to Macao reported: "The Chinas following this coin with such an earnest eagerness as not to be beaten from the place where they know where it is. Offering their commodities to sale with an extraordinary importunity, and they will as soon part with their blood as it, having once possession of it." (C. R. Boxer, The *Vergulde Draeck*, "History Today," Vol. XVIII, 3 March, 1968.) They were accepted throughout Europe, and were official coinage in the early history of the United States until the United States struck its own silver dollars of similar size and value. "The Almighty Dollar," the legal heir of the piece-of-eight, is still the most important monetary unit in the world.

After Hernando Cortez conquered Mexico in 1521, and Pizarro overran the kingdom of the Incas in 1533, the Spanish joyfully understood the enormous value of the wealth accidentally gained through Columbus' abortive attempt to reach the East Indies. Europe was flooded with silver from the New World. Mexico alone has produced more than half the world's silver supply since the capitulation of Montezuma.

One of the remarkable things about the piece-of-eight, the favourite silver piece of privateers and pirates on the Spanish Main, was the way it held its value while European coins underwent constant ups and downs and debasements. Wayte Raymond, in his *Silver Dollars of North and South America*, writes: "The Spanish silver dollar of eight reales . . . maintained an unimpaired integrity throughout its four-century-long history. This is probably an unequalled record among silver coins of the world."

Silver from the slave mines, where the poor Indians hacked, picked, and died, often under the lashes of the overseers. Silver carried by pack-mule to Vera Cruz to be loaded aboard Spanish galleons of the Plate Fleet (from "plata" = money, or silver) which once a year banded in convoy to carry the wealth of the New World to Spain.

From there the wealth was dispersed through Europe to bankers and merchants. Ironically, much of it found its way to enemies of Spain, and was used to pay soldiers and sailors who fought against His Catholic Spanish Majesty. Sometimes the riches were captured before they could reach Europe; looted in the acrid smoke of cannon fire by whooping, grinning, cut-throat privateers—Dutch, English, or French —who liked nothing better than to spit in the eye of the King of Spain and to grow rich on his ill-gotten gains.

The pieces-of-eight—which we still find in ancient shipwrecks today, with the mint marks of Mexico and Peru, and the shear-marks of the old mint masters clear to see after three centuries—had an aura of romance around them which no coins have enjoyed before or since. The rough, glamorous Real de a Ocho established its value when the world was wide and men sailed to death or glory in wooden ships.

The *Zeewyk* men dumped the heavy chests of precious metal and coin on the stony shores of their island, and no doubt looked at each other with silent thoughts of what might be done with the treasure if they, and not the Company, were its masters.

On this island, the silver was useless. It would not buy a seal steak or a drink of water. But in the Indies or Europe it would make many men rich for life.

Some of the hands must have begun to dream of what could be done with the riches if they could break the bonds of their sea prison, and escape. It would have been unnatural if they had not. But no mention of insurrection, or mutiny, or wicked and covetous pawing of the Company's silver is made in van der Graeff's journal. He writes carefully of trips to the reef in the scows and gig, of seals caught, and top-sail breezes, and items unloaded from the ship. And the usual squabbles between men on the wreck and those on the other side of the reef about whether the gap was navigable . . . "The gig returned to the island with nothing but a letter from the master which he had thrown overboard in an empty bottle chest in which he informs the boatswain and the boatswain's mate who were then on the reef, that he and all the men who were on the wreck would not throw overboard a single article or give the same unless we came to the wreck to fetch the goods . . ."

The reply (indignant, and at length): "I the under-merchant Jan Nebbens after the boatswain and the boatswain's mate have again returned without victuals, having read the letter brought from you and understanding therefore that you wish to have us come aboard in spite of the weather and violent surf on the reef, which was impossible as the men tell me, wish that you on board were here on the island to make the 'easy' trip to the wreck. This we the undersigned (signatures of all on the island) declare together. And, Master Steyns, you and your men ought to know that we officers on the island were requested by the hands to issue the wine and the brandy as long as there is any left. The reason being, as you know, that it has not pleased the Good Lord to grant any rain, for it is as dry on the island as it has not been before. The little water which is left in the well is not drinkable, being as salty as sea-water, and this is the cause that there is now no longer any water in the tents. . . ."

By 29 September van der Graeff reported the castaways "at our wits end with thirst." Yet—as fortune had favoured them in the past—luck was once again on their side. Just when it was most needed a well of good fresh water was discovered on the thirtieth, on one of the rocky islands to the south-east. It was to solve their water problems for months. The Most High was very merciful to them.

The argument with the skipper became one of principle. The boats would go to the reef and their crews gaze with exaggerated awe at whatever size breakers might be running that day. The skipper on the wreck, and his men—stamping in anger and frustration just out of earshot—periodically fired guns to emphasize their point, and van der Graeff dutifully scribbled the occurrences in his log. Such as

"September 29th; At dusk a shot was fired at the wreck from which we assume they want us on the reef again."

In the end the skipper and his men made a scow on the wreck and rowed themselves huffily ashore, on 8 October, after having spent nearly a month on board against their will. Steyns' first action on landing was to order van der Graeff and Jan Nebbens to go to the wreck to become the supervising officers, and see how *they* liked living out among the damp and spray. The diary then becomes a daily list of items shipped ashore or floated to the reef. Coming ashore on the twenty-ninth, van der Graeff dropped his journal in the water, and almost wept as the precious pages—those kept during the period on the wreck—drifted away on the current. He had to re-write them from memory.

"Tuesday, October 29: . . . But know this. That in lowering the scow my journal, that is to say the entries made on board the wreck, fell overboard and floated away, so that if anything has been omitted here, which could easily have happened, I would beg indulgence, at least for the time I spent on the wreck."

"From the wreck we have despatched a good deal of victuals to those who came daily to the reef, as well as timber, rope, and iron fittings. Everything, in short, which could serve for the building of a new vessel for our rescue. We have also continued demolishing the forecastle on which a start had been made, as well as the cabin and master's cabin and have made of the planks a large new scow to sail to the reef sending the remainder of the timber to the reef as rafts. Here follows a list of all we despatched from the 10th to the 29th, this being the time I spent on the wreck:

"One chest of carpenter's tools; 49 aums of wine; 1 aum of red wine; 14 rolls of sail cloth; 12 assorted barrels of bread; ½ aum of sweet oil; 63 kegs of butter; 7 cases assorted bacon and meat; 9 rafts of timber; 2 barrels of stock-fish; 7 barrels of bacon and meat; 3 barrels of groats; 4 assorted barrels of brandy; 1 case of Edam cheese; 4 assorted cable; 17 assorted lines; 1 dozen housing; 1 dozen marlin spikes; the ship's bell; the grindstone and tank; the chambers of the swivel guns; 4 bags of nails; 1 set of gudgeons and pintles of a boat. Furthermore a bag of nails was contained in each bread barrel, and we sent off unnumerable small items which have not been mentioned here."

Also sent in the boats were the last of the men who had not previously been ashore; the most determined wreck-hangers such as Pieter de Klerk, the errant lookout. The last man of all was Godvrind Stroomeyer, who went ashore with Nebbens and van der Graeff on 27 October. During van der Graeff's period on the wreck a number of men died. There is no mention of burial. Presumably they were slid over the side with brief ceremony to the waiting sharks who patrolled the breakers at the back of the reef.

On 30 October: "Today we decided to build here in the island a vessel for our rescue, since time is passing by, and help from Batavia which was to have been summoned by our boat can no longer be looked forward to."

They laid the keel of the boat they were to call the *Sloepie*, or "Little Sloop," on 7 November 1727, and in the ensuing weeks (during which van der Graeff complained of scurvy ulcers and a "wound" on his right leg) erected stem post and timbers. A barrel of wine was ceremoniously broached on the keel on the twenty-eighth, to toast good fortune to the new vessel.

Spring had given way to early summer. Calm days with light winds and the corals bright in crystal waters. Glorious days, with the yawl and scows making daily trips to the wreck for materials, and to the mangrove thickets on the long island to cut knees and ribs for the new boat.

With barrels of food piled high on the island, plenty of food, wine, brandy, and fresh water, and the new sloop taking shape nicely under the supervision of carpenter Conrad Snoek and his mates, Andries Cornelissen and Anthony Hybeeck, a mood of general optimism prevailed at the end of the month of November.

The complacency was to be rudely shattered with the first day of the new month, when a blackness descended on the island.

12
The Stupid Sin

THE TWO SODOMY-ACCUSED BOYS WERE DOOMED FROM THE
moment that the eager informants burst into the officers'
tent with the news.

Their shipmates were convinced of their guilt even before
the mockery of the trial, and despite their protestations of
innocence, there was little that could save them from death.

They were accused, tortured, sentenced, and executed.
That was the way of things.

It was a hard and cruel age. In Holland it was an afternoon's entertainment to watch criminals being hanged.
Sometimes there was the additional feature of wretches
having their hands chopped off, being broken on the wheel,
or beheaded, if the authorities thought they merited a
particularly unpleasant exit from this world.

Mutilations, such as branding with a hot iron, hand-
lopping, cropping of ears, splitting of noses or cheeks, were
not infrequently ordered by the magistrates, and torture
was considered to be an entirely reasonable way of getting
the truth from a wrongdoer who was hardly likely to confess

129

of his own free will when he knew what sort of punishment he would receive.

The youths were accused of a homosexual act. The "stupid sin" as the Dutch called it.

"December 1st, 1727: At 8 o'clock in the morning the Petty Officers enter our tent and ask to see the Skipper, and inform him that two hands named Adriaen Spoor, from St. Maertensdyck, and Pieter Engels, from Ghent, both boys, were found yesterday committing together the abominable sins of Sodom and Gomorrah. Which fact cries greatly to Heaven, and distresses the Skipper and other members of the Ship's Council."

"Whereupon the master asked, 'Friends how did you come to know this?' To which they answered, 'Here are three good witnesses who saw it. They will give you proper attestation.'"

"These witnesses were present at once and promised the skipper and Council they would give sworn evidence; being: Frans Feban, quartermaster, and Dirck Jansen van Griecken, quartermaster; Hendrick Armanse, seaman.

"Whose testimony was as follows: 'We, the undersigned Frans Feban, quartermaster, and Dirck Jansen van Griecken, also quartermaster, and Hendrick Armanse, seaman, all in the service of the United East India Company. In our duties as mentioned being present in these islands called by us Fredrik Houtmans. Having come out in the Company's ship *Zeewyk* in the year 1726, and having remained here through the wrecking of the aforesaid ship, hereby do declare at the requisition of Jan Steyns, Skipper, of the service of the same Company and present in the same islands . . . That it is wholly true what happened to us on the 30th of November, 1727; What Abominable and God-forsaken deed was committed by Adriaen Spoor van St. Maertensdyck, and Pieter Engels van Ghent, junior seamen, in that they committed the crime of Sodom and Gomorrah.'"

The witness further declared: "We state this to be the whole truth which we shall at all times and wherever it may be, corroborate willingly by oath."

Jan Nebbens was the official witness to the signatures.

The white-faced boys were brought to the officers' tent, "But they were not willing to make a confession. Wherefore we placed burning fuses between all their fingers. But being obstinate they would no more confess. So upon due consideration we resolved with the entire Council, and the consent of the Common Hands, to place these men apart on one of the northernmost islands."

Marooning, death by exposure. That was what the verdict meant.

To emphasise the official nature of the proceedings van der Graeff wrote evidence and verdict all out again at length, and the result was signed by all the officers and petty officers.

"Inasmuch as following the accusation of 2 quartermasters and a seaman of the Company's late ship *Zeewyk*, now wrecked off the islands named by us Frederik Houtmans, with regard to the persons named Adriaen Spoor, van St. Maertensdyck, junior seaman; and Pieter Engels van Ghent, junior seaman; of the complement of the ship mentioned. It has appeared to us clearly and truthfully that the persons mentioned, on 30th November, 1727, at about 3 o'clock in the afternoon, committed in the island the abominable and God-forsaken deeds of Sodom and Gomorrah, to the great sorrow of the officers, distress of the crew, and general peril of our island. Through which deed terrible plagues may strike our people, or discord may occur among us, with the loss of all that is good. The outrageous and God-forsaken manner of living has reached such a height that the junior seamen did not fear God nor justice in committing the acts. Inasmuch as three persons named Frans Feban, quartermaster, Dirck van Griecken, quarmaster, and Henrick Armanse, seaman, present in this island by accident happened to find these junior seamen doing these abominable deeds. All of which are of a dangerous and evil nature and where justice prevails ought to be punished by death for the prevention of further evil.

"Therefore the full Council of the island mentioned resolved with the greatest speed to place burning fuses between the fingers of these persons to make them confess.

But they, being obdurate, refused to confess. Whereupon we have resolved in council to place them apart from each other on the remotest islands. Which decision has been unanimously reached and approved and have had the junior seamen conveyed to the islands in the yawl on the 2nd day of December, anno 1727. This verdict has been passed, sentenced, announced, and executed by us at Fredrik Houtman, on December 2nd 1727.

Seconded by Jan Nebbens as witness.

Signed: Jan Steyns, Adriaen van der Graeff, Christiaen Radis, David Gossier, Christiaen Melo, Pieter van Ekele, Jan Christiaen Ulrich, Coen Snoeck, Evert Blanck Byle, Jan Pieterse, Jacob Stelle, Jan d'Waeter, Dirck Jansen van Griecken, Frans Feban, Abraham van der Ede, Jacobus van Couwenberghe, Anthony Bybeeck, Jacob Smits."

The boys were rowed across to one of the tiny cays at the north-eastern corner of the island group, about eleven miles away, and set ashore on separate islands. The boat, with an official party of Jan Nebbens the merchant, van der Graeff, the boatswain Christiaen Radis, and six unnamed seamen, then put about and left them to die.

Marooning was a favourite method of getting rid of shipboard troublemakers in the seventeenth and eighteenth centuries. It could take any of a number of forms. Men could be set ashore at ports or places where they would be in no great peril, and where they would be easily able to pick up another ship. They could be given a sporting chance, as Palsaert in 1629 gave Wouter Looes and Jan Pelgrom by leaving them with provisions, a scow, muskets, and goods for trading with the natives—or as was Alexander Selkirk, the original model for Defoe's Robinson Crusoe, when he was similarly left on the Juan Fernandez Islands in 1704. Or it could simply be a grim choice of deaths. A man left on a sand-bar at low tide, with a pistol loaded with one bullet and the choice of drowning at high tide or blowing his brains out. Or stranded on a rock with no chance or choice at all.

Marooning had the advantage that shipmates did not have to spill the blood of men they had lived and messed

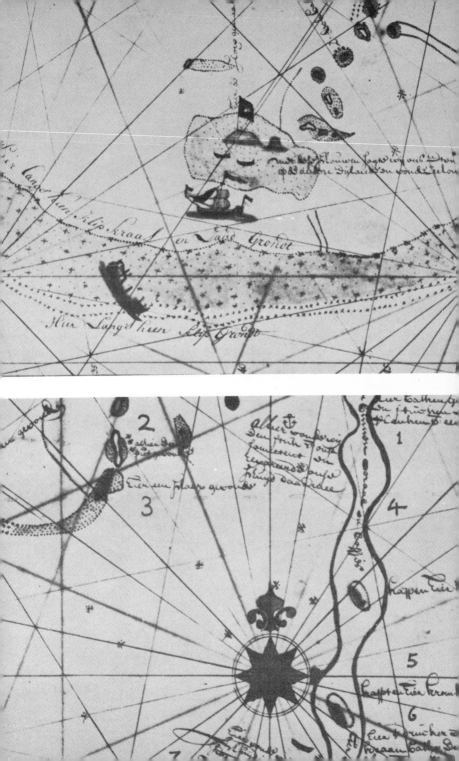

Sondag den 30.e in d'vanagt s'morgens en voor...
de wind Z.Z.O en Z.O maar... C. Elders...
goed weer nademid. s'avonds en in
voornagt de wind Z bramz... C. Elders
... goed weer

December

maandag den 1.e in d'vanagt s'morgens en voorennui
de wind Z bramz... C. Elders...
Dese morgen derden tog 11 Coler balut...
onledue een d'inar... oindrede onder
... monteklent vragtude onder
te mogen opticken. die den skipp... berigt
dat Z personen genaamt...
adriaan spoor van sint in aerlens dyk...
pieter Vugtde van gent...
beide jongue matrosen op gisteren ind...
branden zyn op een god gewldue wyse...
...lyke zonden van sodom en gomorra
...anderen bedryvende 't welk tot de...
skeige enden skipp. benoyng... de per...
skeeps raad een... door door...
gaand daar op de skipp. vraagde...
toe komt gy dat te... en waar de...
woorden lider zyn dits goed getuyge...
... gedien Elden die zullen... daer van

with. Nature provided the final solution. It was very tidy in this respect.

Van der Graeff does not record whether the two wretched boys were left any provisions when they were tumbled ashore. Nor does he mention any conversation in the boats, pleas for mercy, or whether they remained adamant in their story of innocence to the last. His next point of interest, after a vexed comment that they could not reach their own island by nightfall and had to camp out, was the discovery of a mast check from the *Zeewyk*, washed up on "an island lying east of our island."

From this last piece of information it is certain that the boys were marooned on the cays known today as the Mangrove Islands. Mere nodules of coral slates and spikey bushes raised four feet above the surrounding reefs. There is no water on them. No food. Deep channels run between islets and if the boys could not swim they would have been prisoners, each on his own rock until they died from sun and thirst, or went mad with despair and flung themselves in the water. In any event death must have overtaken them within a day or two.

The pages of van der Graeff's journal covering 1 and 2 December, 1727 show the great gap between our time and that of the *Zeewyk* men.

In some superficial ways there are considerable similarities. The *Zeewyk* men, after all, were flesh and blood like ourselves. Their howl of pain and exasperated oaths when a leaf of Old Shin Gasher cabbage coral gave way under their tread, and lacerated their ankles or shins, would have been remarkably similar to those of a 1970 shell collector afflicted in the same way while tramping along the reef.

Their organization—skipper, first, second, and third mates, chaplain, surgeon, boatswain, petty officers, ratings—was virtually identical with that of a modern ship. Their messes, prayers, tents, and everyday way of living would have many familiarities for us, and the dress of shirts and baggy trousers cut off at the knees was not markedly different from that of many fishermen and beachcombers of the present time.

TOP: A portion of the journal kept by Adriaan van der Graeff. This page records the discovery of Adriaen Spoor and Peter Engels "committing the abominable sin of Sodom and Gomorrah. BOTTOM: The wood god Pan grins maliciously from a bronze bo'sun's whistle, found in the sand where the *Zeewyk* survivors camped

But these were skin-deep similarities. The real essence—the attitudes, tolerances (or lack of them) and beliefs were as different from our own age as their own were from the mediaeval.

They held human life cheap from seeing so much death around them. Acts of senseless cruelty were common. Slavery was regarded as a perfectly natural and convenient form of labour. The public humiliation of a wrongdoer in stocks or pillory, or killing of a criminal before a crowd of townsfolk, was an entertainment as well as a moral lesson.

The first sentences passed by Europeans in Australia—punishments of the *Batavia* mutineers ordered by Pelsaert in 1629—included hanging with hand-lopping, marooning, keelhauling, dropping from the yard-arm, and flogging.

In the light of what could have been done to them, perhaps the poor boys of the *Zeewyk* escaped lightly. And yet there are some aspects of the case which indicate that maybe there was more to the whole thing than met the eye. Despite the harsh punishments of the time, homosexuality on board ship was not uncommon. Men deprived of women were quick enough to find substitutes, and the initially forced habits often became ingrained among the older hands. Sex relations between men, however undesirable one may consider them to be, are, and have always been, common in navies and merchant ships, in gaols, and in most exclusively male societies except, perhaps, religious ones. We may gather that the *Zeewyk* men found their outlets.

In the case of the boys, emphasis was placed, in sentencing them, in the brazen nature of the unnatural sexual intercourse in broad daylight. Perhaps it was the flagrant nature of the indiscretion that enraged their shipmates.. There is also the interesting point that Engels, by his own choice, once refused to go back to the island in a boat, and spent a week on his own out on the reef in June in a situation which would seem tantamount to suicide. Though he was rescued he might easily have died in the rough weather at that time, and perhaps he had been driven to it and was hoping for death as a result of bullying or some persecution on the part of his shipmates. Homosexuals or effeminate types are often the butt of bullies, and the marooning that was the black stain on the month of December, may have been a final vicious *coup de grâce* in a prolonged victimization by hypocritical crew-mates.

Bullying, teasing, tormenting, are all too familiar in boarding schools and closed communities of men. Animals in cages, and birds and hens in pens, often exhibit the same unlovely characteristics, driving companion captives to death after weeks of persecution. Possibly the *Zeewyk* men in their open-air prison did the same thing, and it is interesting to note the modern psychological belief that those who are most condemnatory of sexual deviation are often those who sense the desire for such deviation within themselves.

Perhaps from shame or conscience the incident was never mentioned again in van der Graeff's journal, and the islands where the boys were marooned were not noted on the maps of skipper and understeersmen, though almost every other detail—including planks and wheels of gun carriages washed on islands, "bones of a cat's head," and other trivia—were included. There was no reference in any of the later Company correspondence. It was a closed subject.

More than a century later, in 1844, one of a party who had gone to the Abrolhos from the recently established Swan River colony to survey for guano and a fishing industry, laid his groundsheet down in darkness on the Mangrove Islands, and after a wretchedly uncomfortable night got up grumbling in the morning to find he had slept on a human skeleton.

It may have been the pathetic remains of Adriaen Spoor or Pieter Engels.

The skulls, and bones, of many of the other *Zeewyk* men have been turned up in a surprisingly well-preserved condition in the sand dunes of their island. Explorers, guano-diggers, fishermen, oil-drillers, have gaped in their turn at the empty eye sockets and mirthless grins of men who died there in 1727 and 1728. One after another of the Dutchmen turned his shoulder on life, and closed his eyes in the longest sleep. Some died in the scrub of the island, others in their makeshift bunks. Each man had his name and rank recorded in van der Graeff's journal. Nothing more—no account of his service, no description of the man or personality, not even the nature of his illness or injury. Death was too common in the eighteenth century for that. The name was put down simply so that his relatives could be paid his wages up to that day, and not a stuiver more.

Apart from their home-bred knowledge of shallow waters and small boat handling, these coral islands must have seemed a strange world to men fresh from Holland. So different from the cobbled streets of their walled towns, with the open-air fish markets beside the canals, the skaters on the ponds and frozen waterways, the carriages and sleds rattling past. Where a man's breath steamed and smoked in the morning air and he beat his hands together against the cold.

The Dutch were great drinkers and feasters, hearty in toast and song, gamblers of spirit, earnest and efficient even in debauch, and the *Zeewyk* men must have had their merry moments. There were kegs and cases of bottles from the ship's cargo to be consumed among the sandhills. They stuffed their whiskered mouths with sturgeon and salmon intended for the rich burghers and Company officials in Batavia, sucked on long white churchwarden clay pipes and sang around their fires. Dicing and playing cards to pass the time, telling stories of wine and women enjoyed in the misty cold of the Netherlands, so far from these outlandish islands.

Coming from a sentimental nation, the castaways must have felt especial nostalgia at Christmas and New Year, and the traditional times of feasting and dancing in the Netherlands—Martinmas, the Feast of St Nicholas, the times when the Kermis fun-fairs with singing, dancing, beer and laughter in the streets lasting a week or a fortnight, were held.

If they held any celebrations of their own at these times on the island, van der Graeff did not record them. 25 December, in his journal, escaped notice as being Christmas Day except that ten kegs of wine were issued to the hands, with no mention of the reason. New Year is simply announced in the journal as "Anno 1728 in the island."

136

It is true that he was writing in the time-honoured style laid down by the Company, which required all details of information on weather, courses, losses or accidents, important happenings, and the names of dead men. But no random trivia or foolish thoughts. The journal was supposed to be a reference file of sailing and trade information, not a novel or personal diary.

But English ship's journals of the same period, such as the wonderfully rambling and anecdotal jottings of William Dampier, were much more interesting and informative. It is true that a ship's log, dry and factual as van der Graeff's record, was also kept. But the journals were regarded as an equally sacred responsibility. They were often lively accounts of life aboard ship and the events and sightings of a voyage, as is shown by a random extract from the 1788 journal of William "Bully" Bligh—more famous as a martinet than a writer. He was trying to beat the ninety-foot brig *Bounty* east to west around the wintery Horn in January against adverse wind and sea, and having little luck. But he still found time to brace himself against the bucking of the brig and pen such an entry as, "The stormy weather continued with a great sea. The ship now began to complain and required to be pumped every hour, which was no more than we had reason to expect from such a continuance of gales of wind and high seas. The decks also became so leaky that I was obliged to alot the great cabin of which I had made little use, except in fine weather, to those people who had wet berths to hang their hammocks in; and by this means the 'tween decks was less crowded.

"Every morning all the hammocks were taken down from where they hung and when the weather was too bad to keep them upon deck they were put in the cabin; so that the 'tween decks were cleaned daily and aired with fires if the hatchways could not be opened. With all this bad weather we had the additional mortification to find at the end of every day that we were losing ground; for not-withstanding our utmost exertions and keeping to the most advantageous tacks (which, if the weather had been at all moderate, would sufficiently have answered our purpose) yet the greater part of the time we were doing little better than drifting before the wind.

"Birds as usual were about the ship, and some of them caught; and for the first time since we left Staten Land we saw some whales. This morning owing to the violent motion of the ship the cook fell and broke one of his ribs and another man, by a fall, dislocated his shoulder. The gunner, who had charge of a watch, was laid up by the rheumatism, and this was the first sick-list that appeared on board the ship. The time of full moon which was approaching made me entertain hopes that we should experience some change of wind or weather in our favour. But the event did not answer our expectations. The Latitude at Noon this day was 58 deg. 9 min. S., and Longitude 76 deg. 1 min. W."

"We caught a good many birds. . . . A great many of these were frequently about the wake of the ship, which induced the people to float a line with hooks baited to endeavour to catch them, and their attempts were successful. The method they used was to fasten the bait a foot or two before the hook and by giving the line a sudden jerk when the bird was at the bait it was hooked in the feet or body. . . . Were all lean and tasted fishy, so we tried an experiment on them which succeeded admirably. By keeping them cooped up and cramming them with ground corn they improved wonderfully in a short time; so that the pintada birds became as fine as ducks, and the albatrosses were as fat and not inferior in taste to fine geese. Some of the latter birds that were caught measured 7 ft. between the extremities of the wings. . . ."

The superstition that the albatrosses, or "sea-mews," were spirits of dead mariners, and that it was ill-luck to hurt one, apparently belonged to later clipper crews. Certainly Bligh's was an ill-omened voyage, culminating in the final disaster of the mutiny. But it was well-narrated in his journal, and one wishes van der Graeff had shown similar talent or industry with his seagull quill pen. Van der Graeff, whose name, by ironic coincidence, means "to write," in its original Graeco-Latin derivation, seldom gives any colour or emotion to his account.

138

There are exceptions, such as the first night on the wreck or when the thick-tongued panic of a thirsty man breaks through the official jottings. . . . "We are at our wits end for water!" . . . But in the main he is remarkably and consistently pedantic. Four times a day—for each of the watches normally kept aboard ship—wind and weather were noted and chronicled: "Reefed topsail breeze . . . clear sky with scud . . . topgallent breeze, good weather . . ." and the like.

But when the boy Pieter Grounewoud is found face-down in the centre of the island he is simply, "Found dead in the scrub," without a word about how his young life left him. New Year arrives without a remark such as "We hardly expected to be here when we left the Netherlands thirteen months ago, but we are making the best of it and are hopeful of a favourable outcome." Deadpan van der Graeff simply noted the brisk easterly wind which blew in the year 1728 as being "a reefed topsail breeze" and after noting the wind-shifts of the other "watches" during the fine but breezy weather of the day, let it go at that.

Perhaps we should be grateful that we have the journal at all. We can at least fill in the gaps with background knowledge and catch occasional revealing glimpses from its pages. But it would have been wonderful if, just once or twice, the man had been human and really written what he saw and felt instead of clerking for the Honourable Company as a dull, dumb, bounden duty.

So much of human experience which would have been interesting and perhaps valuable for later generations has been lost through history.

Usually it is the simplest things, those taken for granted, which are overlooked—routine shipboard tasks like lowering boats, taking soundings, raising an anchor, all arts in themselves—and years later we wonder how they did it. Probably our descendants will wonder how people of the first forty years or so of this century rode horses, lit an oil lamp, saddled a camel, or ploughed a furrow with a team.

Van der Graeff could have written a marvellous castaway's handbook, valuable to sailors of his own time and later, and of tremendous interest to historians in succeeding centuries. But he didn't, and more's the pity.

On the day following his return from marooning the two boys he has his quill out and is writing: "December 4th; In the late night, morning, and forenoon, the wind SSW, topsail breeze, clear sky, good weather. At 7 o'clock in the morning the boatswain goes to the reef with the two scows. Today we inspect the victuals and store in a separate tent as many victuals as we think we shall require for the voyage to Batavia, these goods being those on the following list."

Conscientiously he scratches lists of leaguers of bread, aums of oil, brandy, and wine, barrels of butter and groats, casks of cheese. Grog and groceries. Van der Graeff was at his best making lists. He was a natural storekeeper, and perhaps he lived to become one with the money he made from the sea.

Meantime the men were despatched to the reef for victuals and timber from the part-demolished wreck, for knees from the big mangroves on the long island, for seals and water from the rocky islets to the south east . . . the routines which were all aimed at the one target, escape!

13
The Little Sloop

THEY CALLED THEIR VESSEL *Sloepie*, A TERM OF AFFECTION for the little sloop which was to be their deliverance from the world of the dead. Under the direction of the carpenter and his mates, they built her strong and beamy to carry more than eighty men, three tons of treasure, and several tons of water and provisions. Stout to weather the roughest seas they might encounter between their island of "Fredrik Houtman" and Indonesia, their point of safety.

Nearly two thousand miles of ocean lay between them and their goal. Smaller boats had sailed longer distances, but there was always the element of luck, and like all good sailors they prepared for the worst and hoped for the best.

Smiling seas and fresh favourable winds might make a picnic of the voyage. Or — God forbid! — they might encounter a late cyclone, with winds and waves big enough to make an Indiaman fight for her life, let alone their smaller vessel.

They took every precaution, making fastenings double-strength, and building mighty ribs and knees into her at

141

points where waves make their greatest test of a boat. She was between fifty and sixty feet long with a beam of seventeen to twenty feet, and drew a fathom, or six feet of water when fully laden.

She would have been typical of the sturdy fishing craft that the Dutch knew how to build and sail so well. They had had centuries of experience of fishing the dirty waters of that treacherous, turbulent piece of water, the North Sea, for herring, cod, and lobster, and the Zeeland men were among the best small craft builders and seamen in the Netherlands.

The *Sloepie* was the first ocean-going vessel built in Australian history, and the first to incorporate native timbers. For though she was mainly built of stout oak and Baltic pine from the poor *Zeewyk*, many of her ribs and knees were taken from the stand of big mangroves on the Long Island. She also incorporated pieces of the stranger—the unknown wreck which they had found when they arrived on the islands as reluctant visitors.

Few boats could have been built of better materials. The weathered and sea-tested timbers from the *Zeewyk* and the unknown wreck were the best available to the shipyards of Europe. The East Indiamen hulls were built of oak— pieces known as "Rhine straights"—shipped down the Rhine by barge from German forests. Their ribs and knees were also oak. The pine planking for the decks came from the black forests of the Baltic where wolves howled through the long nights. The masts were fashioned from the firs which grew straight and tall in Norway. The whole framework and fabric of the ship was pinned together with "tree-nails"; pegs turned from iron-hard knots of Irish oak. All the European timber was winter cut, when the sap was dormant.

Coenrad Snoek had his choice of all these materials from timber aboard the *Zeewyk* on the reef, and what had been brought ashore in rafts or washed up. The native mangrove knees, to which they also had recourse, were by no means inferior. Pearling luggers on the north-west coast of Western Australia have used mangrove knees for nearly a century. The close-grained wood is renowned for its endurance.

The *Sloepie* also had choice of compasses, charts, and all the *Zeewyk's* navigation instruments. There were masts, spars, sails, strops, dead-eyes, chains, cables, anchors, and running gear enough to fit out two such vessels as they were building. She even had the *Zeewyk's* bell, brought ashore on 29 October, and for armament they were able to take the light quick-firing bronze swivel guns from her poop, in case they should have to protect their ten chests of treasure from native pirates when they reached the Indies. Two were brought in the scows on 4 December for this purpose.

There was nothing they lacked. It was simply a question of time and care to do the job well, courage to make the voyage, and commonsense to choose their time of sailing for the best weather.

Skipper Jan Steyns drew a picture of the *Sloepie* on his map of the islands, and the original is preserved in the East India Company archives in The Hague today. It shows a stout little ship with a single mast, and two square-rigged sails and a jib. There is a raised poop or after cabin. A pennant flies from the masthead, and a huge red-white-and-blue Netherlands flag, several sizes too big, drapes from a post at the stern. Clearly they had considerable pride in her.

The Swedish naval architect and shipbuilder, Frederick Hendrik af Chapman, whose illustrated work *Architectura Naval Mercatoria* is the standard authority on the lines and dimensions of eighteenth century shipping, has drawings of all the Dutch merchant and fishing craft in meticulous detail. The line drawings of an East Indiaman in his 1768 book show a merchantman identical to the *Zeewyk*, except that the sail plan had by this time been belatedly changed to include a jib instead of the square "blind" sail at the end of the bowsprit. All the ship's boats, including the longboat like the craft in which Langeweg and his picked men tried tragically to sail to Batavia, the smaller and neater yawl which was so useful for sealing and exploring around the islands, and the flat-bottomed scows, shallow-draft punts, or "flatties" which they used for scouting over the reef shallows, are depicted in his pages, with descriptions, dimensions, draughts, armaments, and crew numbers. The book is a mine of eighteenth-century maritime information.

His illustrations show a number of vessels called "sloops" and "yachts" ranging from forty to sixty-six feet in length. A privateering sloop, for example, was listed as carrying a crew of fifty men, and ten swivel guns. She was sixty-two feet long, twenty feet in the beam, and had a seven-and-a-half feet draught. This was the bulk and muscle needed for a craft like the *Sloepie*. To lift her weight of men, money, and provisions, a forty-foot boat would have been too small. Anything much over sixty feet would have been too difficult to handle at the launching. This was the biggest initial problem with the *Sloepie*. Selecting a convenient building site which would enable her to be roller-launched and floated into the shallows caused furrowed brows and a good deal of argument and counter-argument among the Dutchmen. There were no easy or obvious launching sites because of the shallow water around all the islands. They must have inspected many possible places, on their own and nearby islets, before they compromised on a sloping rock on the easternmost extremity of their own island. There was barely four feet of water at its foot, but on top tides they could count on a little more, and Coenrad Snoek, the head carpenter, must have reasoned that if the hull was launched part-completed and unballasted she would float high. Four feet or so of green water would be enough to move her to a depth where they could continue building her sides up in deeper water. If she grounded lightly it was a sandy bottom, and no great harm could be done.

They laid her keel on 7 November 1727. It took them four months to build her. Some of the men worked on her hull under the direction of Coenrad Snoek, while others were sent out to cut knees from wreck-wood and mangroves (they cut a total of 117 knees overall), or to get beams, timbers, ropes, blocks, brasswork and running gear from the *Zeewyk*, on the reef. They had plenty of time to think about the coming voyage. Their deadliest danger was the cyclones which brew and brood off the North West Australian coast in the baking summer months. Occasionally they erupt in spinning air masses, to become shrieking furies with winds

144

up to 120 miles per hour, scything and destroying everything in their path. Pearling luggers, coastal vessels, and even large steamships have disappeared in exceptional cyclones, and they parallel in viciousness and fury the hurricanes of the Caribbean and Florida coasts or the typhoons of the China Sea.

The accepted cyclone period is from Christmas to the end of March, though occasional mavericks appear out of season. The cyclone belt extends across the tropics and sub-tropic areas of the Indian Ocean, with favourite hunting grounds off the northern Australian coast and around the islands of Cocos, Mauritius, and Madagascar. Ships of the East India Company were forbidden to sail from Batavia to the Cape of Good Hope in the period between Christmas and April for fear of them, and it is likely that *Zeewyk* skipper Jan Steyns had the possibility of cyclones in mind when he made his sailing plan. There were other dangers as well; lack of wind, the opposite of cyclones, leading to thirst and scurvy; pirates, uncharted reefs, and all the usual hazards of the day and age at sea.

It was encouraging to remember that smaller craft had made successful voyages from the Southland to Batavia, backed by courage, desperation, and luck. Especially luck.

Some had got through by the skin of their teeth. Others, like their own ship's boat with Pieter Langeweg and his crew, were never heard of again. The journal kept by Abraham Loeman van Santwits (Sandwich), an Englishman serving with the VOC, illustrates the hardships of castaways in little boats. He and fourteen men were given up for lost on the Southland coast in bad weather in 1658, while their ship, the *Waeckende Buoy*, was searching for the *Gilt Dragon* survivors. Undaunted, he sailed for Batavia in a cockleshell boat with the sides built up with seal-skins. They had favourable winds, but soon enough Leeman was writing: "We now have nothing to eat but dry seal meat which is as tough as rope yarn. The men have begun to stop eating, having no appetite because of terrible thirst. We have two or three shells out of which we drink our rations, and when a drop was spilled we regret this exceedingly. Our thirst is too terrible. When one or the other wants to make water he does this in the bailer in a shell, lets it sometimes stand to cool a while. At once someone is at it and trying to drink it so that they fall into an argument and would exchange blows. . . . Everything is so miserable that it is hard to describe. Many have grown so weak that they wanted to lie down all the time, but since we have to bail constantly I cannot permit this and those who will not bail I refuse to give more than a dram of water. On April 19 one man died who constantly called for water, but I could not and dared not help him. At night I hang a cloth in the rigging to be moistened by the dew so that we can suck at it. We frequently wet our bodies so that the moisture can be absorbed . . .

"We have made good progress all the time, and at night I set a course by the stars and sail on in the name of God. But there is no end to the men groaning and wailing of thirst."

On 26 April 1658: "Two of our men have died in great distress, never ceasing to call for a drink before they died, but we could give them no consolation. They had to do with their ration as the others did. . . ."

29 April 1658: "We had only one or two rations of water left and I was very oppressed not knowing how we should carry on and ordered each man to look out well saying, to hearten them, that we were not far from the land of Java. By a miracle in the afternoon the man at the helm sighted land and there was much joy and we became as if new men. . . . Then we had drunk our own water for 16 days and nights and my own mouth and tongue were so rough I could hardly speak because of the burning caused by my own water."

They were overjoyed at the sight of land—another two days at sea would have seen them all dead—but they were far from being saved. Though only four of the fourteen died on the sea voyage, only three of the remainder, including the indomitable Leeman, reached Batavia and safety. The others became lost in the jungle after landing, and died of exposure or were murdered by natives. Leeman and his two companions were held prisoner for several weeks, but were eventually turned over to the Dutch authorities at the

146

intercession of a Javanese prince. Leeman wrote "We came to Batavia as joyful as if we were going to Heaven . . . after that terrible journey, for which deliverance Almighty God must be thanked and praised everlastingly."

A more famous voyage to Batavia was the one made by William Bligh in the longboat of H.M.S. *Bounty*, after the infamous mutiny of 1789. With nineteen men, the small craft was so overloaded that it only had seven inches of freeboard, but Bligh, sustained by his iron will and his determination to be revenged on the mutineers, made a few days' rations last for forty-seven days, and still had some in hand when he reached the Dutch settlement at Kupang on the south western corner of Timor.

The 3,600 miles were sailed and the incredible hardships endured without the loss of a man from thirst or hunger. The only death was quartermaster John Norton, who was murdered by natives in the ironically-named "Friendly" Islands at the start of the voyage. But, like Leeman's crew, the health of many of the men was broken by the ordeal and seven of the eighteen died before they reached England. Bligh wrote of their arrival in Timor before taking a schooner to Batavia: "An indifferent spectator would have been at a loss which most to admire; the eyes of famine sparkling at the immediate prospect of relief, or the horror of the preservers at the sight of so many spectres, whose ghastly countenances, if the cause had been unknown would have excited terror rather than pity. Our bodies were nothing but skin and bones, our limbs were full of sores, and we were clothed in rags. In this condition, with the tears of joy and gratitude flowing down our cheeks the people of Timor beheld us with a mixture of horror, surprise and pity."

Compared with Bligh, the *Zeewyk* men were fortunate castaways. They had a fine big boat, an ample stock of barrelled provisions, and luxuries like wine and brandy. They sailed their escape route like first-class passengers over the leagues of ocean where earlier Dutchmen had struggled for mere existence or expired wretchedly.

As soon as the keel was laid, van der Graeff's journal took on a note of confident optimism. The querulousness,

147

quarrels, and naked aggressions of July and August were gone. The entries of December 1727 and early New Year 1728 depict men moving briskly and purposefully towards a goal. The ship taking shape on the foreshore of their island was a visible symbol of progress.

There were still deaths and burials, with men dying every week in a manner which seems hard to reconcile with the healthy environment of the Abrolhos, but in that age death was familiar and casually accepted. It was the will of God. They dug the graves, wrote the names in the register for stoppage of pay to relatives, and went on with their other appointed tasks.

There were the usual camp quarrels—mainly among the soldiers about the mounting of the guard over the stores—but they were routine matters with none of the smouldering discontent, the seeds of mutiny, of six months previously. When the guard soldiers were found stealing wine they were flogged, and no-one thought any more about it.

On 19 February, when the hull on which he had worked so hard was nearing completion, the carpenter's mate Andries Cornelissen died. For him the *Sloepie* was an epitaph, not a deliverance. By 27 February, with summer hard, hot, and well advanced, they were ready for the launching. "Today we place our vessel on rollers and water-test her, finding her reasonably tight and reeve the gins around the vessel to launch her tomorrow with God's blessing."

On the following day: "At sunrise we commence the launching of our vessel, and by noon have her water-borne through God's gracious help and aid, so that this evening three barrels of wine were consumed in the shipyard." A proper celebration.

They were restless to be away. The comforts, the remembered familiar things of the world of their own kind were calling strongly. The warm musky scent of a woman, the fragrance of kitchen-cooked food, the softness of a bed. Things they once took for granted, and which now seemed to them the very pleasures of Heaven.

They had been on this rock too long. Haste the preparations, speed the loading, hoist the sails for Batavia, and

Top: A poop gun from the *Zeewyk*, with the VOC stamp on its barrel, recovered on the reef in 1968. Bottom: Pieces-of-eight from the bones of a Dutch ship on the coast of Western Australia. The survivors perished miserably long ago, but the rough coins are almost unmarked by the centuries

farewell to the miserable Southland; the prison islands of Frederick Houtman. They drank hungry toasts to home things, boasted greedily of the feats they would accomplish in tavern and brothel in Batavia, and looked longingly at the northern horizon.

On 3 March, van der Graeff took the yawl to scout a passage to the open sea for their sloop, writing a self-important and pompous account in the journal. "At 9 o'clock in the morning I set out from the island in the yawl to seek a passage through which with God's blessing we might be able to reach the sea in our yacht, in which I was extremely successful, since I immediately made up the following plan. Firstly we round the small reef which extends westwards from the NW corner of our island; being clear of all this we shall set our course NE by N until we see the high sandhill of our island bearing S of us, it then being at a distance of about ½ mile. Then we are able to shape a course N until the northernmost surf of our reef is to our WNW, whereupon the course shall be NW until the wreck of the late company ship *Zeewyk* enters the northernmost surf, being then SW by S of us. Then we are to sail WSW under the N side of the reef through which we can plumb our way and shall be able to pass it at 7 or 8 fathoms of water until the high sandhill of our island shall bear SE and the wreck mentioned before S by E. Whereupon we shall be in the open sea and able to set what course we desire."

One wonders whether van der Graeff spent as long looking for a passage as he did writing of his endeavours. He gave them a bad course which could have wrecked them. The route he plotted took the newly-built *Sloepie* perilously close to breaking reefs, and on their way out of the Abrolhos they swamped and lost the yawl which they were towing astern. It was unnecessary for them to "plumb," i.e. feel their way by casting the lead to find the depths of water, through any reefs at all. If they had set a course north-east from their island they could have moved into fifteen and twenty-one fathoms without risk, before turning for the open sea with many fathoms of safe water under their keel. But no-one from the Honourable Company was going to sail to the

TOP: "Drink and the devil have done for the rest." This skull of a *Zeewyk* survivor lay in a high sandhill on the island until it was found more than two centuries after the wreck. BOTTOM: The site on Gun Island where the *Zeewyk* men built the *Sloepie*

accursed desolation of the Australian coast to see whether an understeersman had done a good job or not, and it read prettily enough as penned by van der Graeff.

But imagine if they had lost the sloop as they sailed out . . . the awful despair of the survivors washed back to their island to begin again!

It did not happen that way. Fortune smiled on the *Zeewyk* men in their final weeks, and everything, including the departure, went well for them. They finished decking the *Sloepie* on 4 March; brought her into six feet of water on the west side of the island on the ninth, loaded the Company's money chests on the sixteenth, and stepped the mast on the same day. Haste, more haste . . .

By the twentieth, they were loading stores and bending sails. On the twenty-first they fitted the rudder, and on the twenty-third the officers and most of the hands went aboard. A roll call on 24 March showed that eighty-eight of the original 208 who sailed aboard the *Zeewyk* were still alive.

On Friday, 26 March, "The wind SE by E, reefed mainsail breeze, clear sky, good weather. At 7 o'clock in the morning we weighed anchor and sailed out to sea precisely as noted on the 3rd inst., setting our compasses at 5 deg. E the needle. At midday we observed the wreck of our late ship *Zeewyk* bearing due East at 3½ miles, which wreck is located on the Company's Mercator charts at South Latitude 28 deg. 50 min., Longitude 128 deg. 9 min. Whereupon we set our course W. and at 4 o'clock in the afternoon NW."

They were clear of the reefs, and for the first time in 10 months they were back on the familiar deep blue waters of the open sea. Their hearts must have been light and happy. Salvation was at hand, and over the horizon lay all the things they had yearned for during the long months when they thought they would leave their bones on the barren shores of the islands of Frederick Houtman. Van der Graeff, the unromantic, makes no mention of it, but they would have been inhuman if there had been no celebration.

It would have been interesting to have been on board to watch the faces and hear the thoughts expressed . . . *Sloepie* the new-born sailing out past the wreck of the *Zeewyk*, the dead mother on the reef.

It must have been a moment that each man would remember for as long as he lived. A milestone. One of those rare times when a man's thoughts run strange and deep, and we perceive truths normally hidden from us. A moment when our frail mortality is almost unbearably apparent. The caprice of Fate which allowed some to escape, and dictated that others should remain on the island for ever, seems a little terrifying. Those who sailed away that day must have thanked God with some fervour as the wreck and the sandy line of the island disappeared below the horizon. Gone from their lives forever.

And once they were gone, and they had a heaving deck below their feet again, the familiar sound of the wind in the rigging, the sails standing out strong and full from the masts, many of them must have shaken their heads and wondered if it had all really happened. It may have seemed like a dream, a ten-month unreality, already misting mirage-like in the memory.

14
A Glass to Your Health

THERE WAS A CLATTER OF ARMS IN THE GUARD ROOM AT Batavia castle; an air of unusual excitement. Soldiers buckled on their sword-belts and bandoliers, took pikes from the wooden racks around the wall, and eased on helmets and breastplates.

Two words flew around the guard room and the soldiers' quarters at the castle. They were *Zeewyk* . . . and *Mutiny!*

It was not long before the rumour had flashed around the town. Though the *Batavia* mutiny had occurred a century before, it was still remembered for its grisly horror. Now here was another shipwreck on the same islands, another mutiny, if the reports were correct. If they were true there would be men broken on the wheel, bodies hanging on the town gibbets. The wrath of the Company towards servants who stole its goods and silver, or looted during a shipwreck, was implacable. Mutiny was a crime punishable by the very severest penalties.

The whole town was agog, as the soldiers marched down to the Canal-side and were rowed out to waiting ships which would take them to where the blackguards' vessel—a yacht or sloop ingeniously constructed from wreck timbers—had been arrested in the Straits of Sunda.

No doubt the hangman of Batavia, who like his fellow masters of high works in Holland was paid by piece rates, brightened up at the prospect of considerable addition to his income. Probably he began checking over his gear, with attention given to instruments such as the rods for breaking men's bones when they were spread-eagled on the wheel, the loops, harnesses, pincers, brands, and cutters, which might be needed for the kind of torture befitting mutineers.

The governor, Mattheus de Haan, had been shown the note which caused the uproar. There was no signature, but it was in Jan Steyns' handwriting and had been smuggled out to another ship at Sunda Straits. The writing was shaky but the message was unmistakable:

"My High Excellency, together with the Council of the Netherlandish India, I pray of you most urgently to send me help and assistance against these robbers of the money and goods among themselves. I am stark naked; they have taken everything from me. O my God! They have behaved like wild beasts to me and everyone is master. Worse than beasts do they live and it is impossible that on board a pirate ship things can be worse than here because everyone thinks he is rich from the highest to the lowest of my subordinates. They say among themselves 'Let us drink a glass to your health, ye old ducats!' I am ill and prostrate with scurvy. . . ."

Small wonder that the soldiers were sent marching with grim tread, while the fiscal advocates prepared their quills and parchments for the evidence which they expected would send the mutineers to richly-deserved public execution, the Governor scowled darkly, and the townsfolk of Batavia— bored with ordinary routines, gossip, and the daily drudgery of working for the Company—looked forward eagerly to the return of the troops with the villains in chains. The trials and eventual executions would provide some interest for a week or two.

In the taverns that night they talked of nothing else.

The secretary of the Council of India, J. J. Henriks, sat up with quill and inkwell and a lanthorn writing a report which he titled: "EXTRACT FROM THE DELIBERATIONS AND RESOLUTIONS IN THE COUNCIL OF INDIA, April 26, 1728.

"At five o'clock this afternoon we received a letter by the patchialang vessel *De Veerman*, very unexpectedly and fortunately, from the former skipper and undermerchant of the ship *Zeewyk*, bound for these parts, written in the Straits of Sunda, but undated, reporting the wreck of the ship on the reef lying before the islands Frederick Houtman's Abrolhos, near the Southland, at 28 degrees L., on the 9th of June of last year. The crew having afterwards fetched several necessaries from the wreck, made from the timber a sloop or vessel, on board of which eighty-two souls have reached these straits, together with the money taken out by the ship, consisting of three tons, according to the double (duplicate) invoice received.

"But, besides that letter, there also came to hand a little card, unsigned, apparently in the handwriting of the skipper, in which he complains in unmistakable terms of the behaviour of the crew so that we cannot but suppose that the money chests have been broken open, in order that so splendid a booty might be divided.

"Therefore, on the motion of the Governor-General, it was resolved to send out at once to the assistance of the suffering vessel and crew, who were obliged, in default of fresh water, to put up with salt water for some time.

"Accordingly the brigantine *De Hoop*, and the sloop *De Olyftack*, and the patchialangs *De Snip* and the before named *Veerman*, being made ready by order of his excellency, the advocate-fiscal of India, Mr. Jacob Graafland, with two commissioners from the Council of Justice, assisted by the secretary and usher, together with one sergeant, two corporals, and twelve private soldiers, were dispatched, in order that the ready money might be secured without delay, as much of it, that is, as might still be found.

"Further, a thorough search was to be made after the remainder, both among the crew and in all the corners and nooks of the sloop, which has been put together by them.

"This said sloop no other vessels shall be allowed to approach, with the sole exception of that on board of which the commissioners are; so that all possibility may be removed from any clandestine transfer of the stolen booty to another crew, and of the noble company's being thus injured by a complot of a gang of expert thieves.

"The guilty ones shall be seized and subjected to an exemplary punishment, as a warning to all other evil doers in similar lamentable and fatal occurrences.

J. J. Hendricks, Secr."

Four days later they were back, the four escort vessels bringing the "mutineers'" sloop to anchor with them in Batavia Roads on 30 April. The townsfolk who pressed eagerly to the shore were disappointed to see that no one was brought ashore in chains. In fact the crew of the *Zeewyk* walked about very much like free men, mingling with the soldiers, and showing every joyful anticipation of coming ashore. They certainly did not have the look of mutineers about to get their just deserts.

Soon enough there was a new story about the town. The ship had been lost by the carelessness of the skipper Jan Steyns, who was at present suffering paranoic delusions from scurvy, and ranting that his command and goods had been stolen from him. But in fact the crew had not only salvaged the Company's money chests from the wreck on the reef, they had brought them complete according to invoice to Batavia, in the vessel which they had constructed from wreck wood with courage and fortitude on the lost islands.

They were men back from the dead, and rightly in a mood to celebrate their return to the living. All of them, that is, but the wretched skipper, who would surely have to account for his actions and false accusations.

Human nature running its normal course, the townsfolk now became as eager to celebrate with the new heroes as they had been previously to see them hanged. For several days the *Zeewyk* sailors strutted and swaggered the taverns of Batavia, telling their tale and catching up on all the pleasures and debauches they had been denied during their ten months' sojourn on the grim Southland beach.

Meantime the authorities were faced with unexpected problems. Far from finding money missing from the *Zeewyk*'s inventory, the search by the soldiers and fiscal advocates had produced too much.

The ten chests of treasure of the *Zeewyk*, were complete according to invoice. But in addition to this, other money was found. Some of it was a parcel of 207 Spanish pieces-of-eight and ten schellingen, which the skipper had been given at the start of the voyage to purchase provisions at the Cape of Good Hope, and had secretly saved, presumably for his personal profit. There were also packets of private money found on individual crewmen, which they may have been smuggling on their own behalf or as agents of other people to capitalize on the favourable exchange rate in the Indies.

The large silver ducaton or Rix dollar, the most important coin in Holland and officially worth only sixty-six stuivers in the Netherlands, was actually worth seventy-eight stuivers in exchange in the Indies. Smuggling ducatons from the mother country to the Indies was a profitable racket, and enterprising Company servants brought so many to Batavia that they created a shortage in the mother country. Proclamations were made, edicts passed, penalties imposed to stop the flow. But the smuggling continued. The *Zeewyk* officers and crew were no exception. Steyns had 730 ducatons on his person, the merchant Jan Nebbens 600, and the sailors and soldiers lesser amounts, but totalling more than 5,000 Rix dollars. On the face of it there appeared to be a strong case for confiscation of the illegally-imported money and punishment of the culprits. But Jacob Graafland, the fiscal advocate or Attorney-General at Batavia, had an unusually human streak for those harsh times, and there were aspects which troubled him. In the first place it would be difficult to prove exactly who owned the packages of money, since the names and addresses on them had been obliterated either deliberately by the men themselves, or by water and wear and tear after the wrecking of the *Zeewyk*. Some men may have brought their own genuine savings with them, and would thus be unfairly treated in any general confiscation.

And even the questionable money had been salvaged at

considerable personal risk—as had the Company's treasure—by the crew. The advocate was of the opinion that the sailors ought to be allowed some salvage. The matter was put before Governor and Council for consideration.

Meanwhile, inquiries into Steyns' allegations of mutiny had produced no evidence to substantiate his claims. The crew stood solidly together in questioning. The journal of the steersman Adriaen van der Graeff recorded as the sole untoward incident the falling overboard and drowning of the Scottish third mate Joris Forkson at noon on 13 April—an unlucky day indeed for him—and so close to safety.

There had been a problem about who was to take his watch, and when the third mateship was offered to the bo'sun's mate David Gossier he had gruffly declined, and eventually it had been taken by seaman Robert van der Swaen.

It was true that there had been some breaches of discipline on the islands. Fighting among the soldiers, petty thefts and the like. But they had been punished by flogging according to law, and the breaches were not sufficiently serious to warrant retrial at this late stage. The two death-by-exposure homosexual boys were never mentioned, perhaps in case the plagues and abomination of the wrath of God should belatedly fall, or because of general shame about the matter.

Secretary Henriks, at the direction of Governor de Haan and the members of the Council of India in Batavia, the senior VOC officials who made the executive decisions on important matters, wrote a lengthy report which covered most of the aspects of the *Zeewyk* case, addressing it to the Most High Seventeen, the directors of the VOC in the Netherlands.

TO THE DIRECTORS OF THE ASSEMBLY OF THE SEVENTEEN, On the 26th of April a letter unexpectedly came to hand by the patchialang *De Veerman*, from the late skipper and under-merchant of the Zeeland ship *Zeewyk*, Jan Steyns and Jan Nebbens, written from the Straits of Sunda, but without date communicating the fact that this vessel, after leaving the Cape of Good Hope on the 21st of April, had been wrecked, on the 9th of June, on the reef lying before the islands Frederick Houtman's Abrolhos, situated near the Southland, in S. lat. 29 degrees, and otherwise called the Tortelduyff's Islands.

The crew had, in favourable weather, succeeded in recovering all kinds of necessaries from the wreck, and had constructed from the fragments of the ship a vessel, on which, setting out the 22nd of March, they arrived in the above straits on the 21st of April, numbering eighty-two souls, and bringing with them the moneys of the Company contained in ten chests to the value of Fl. 315,836 : 1 : 8.

All this will more clearly appear from the subjoined copy of the letter (together with a list of the survivors, their names and rank on board before the wreck), to which we respectfully refer you, as also to an extract from the resolution passed on that day.

From this will also be seen the care shown by us for the recovery of the money, in our despatching at once to the distressed vessel (which was suffering from want of fresh water) the advocat-fiscal of India, Mr. Jacob Graafland, with two commissioners from the Council of Justice, assisted by the secretary and usher of the court, provided with the necessary vessels, together with one sergeant, two corporals, and twelve privates, and there was also found a small slip, without signature, written by the skipper, in which he complains of the outrageous behaviour of the crew, so that we could not but conclude that some of the company's chests must have been broken open, and the contents stolen, as it very frequently happens under such unfortunate circumstances.

Wherefore the above-mentioned commissioners were duly instructed to take means to prevent the concealment of the Company's moneys. But the precaution proved unnecessary, as they arrived here happily on the 30th, to the great relief of the Company's heavy losses of money, with the above-mentioned vessel and the ten money chests, which were found to be complete according to the invoice. In addition to this was also received a small bag, containing two hundred and seven pieces of Spanish reals, handed over by the Directors of the Chamber, Middelburg, in Zeeland, to the officers of this ship, for the purchase of fresh provisions, which also was saved.

Moreover various sums in silver ducats, as specified in the memorial, a copy of which is subjoined, were found upon the crew. On that same day, namely, the 30th April, the advocat-fiscal was instructed to report to the government as to whether an action could be brought by it against the pretended owners, who had fetched that money out of the wreck, the fact of their having it in their possession being in our opinion a violation of the law which forbids the export of coined money to private persons.

His answer is to be found in a copy subjoined. But afterwards he was obliged, as a matter of official duty, to put the law in force, and an indictment was accordingly issued against the claimants before the Council of Justice, whose decision is still pending. We are nevertheless of the opinion that salvage ought to be allowed to the men who, at no inconsiderable danger to themselves, brought the money from the wreck.

The journals kept on the voyage, as far as they were saved and brought over, were, in accordance with the resolution of the 30th of April, handed over to the Equipagemeester, Coenrad Mels, and a committee of skippers, under the presidency of the above-mentioned fiscal, as it appeared to us rather doubtful whether the ship had not been wrecked in an inexcusable manner. And, indeed, it was subsequently proved by the report of the committee, that the former skipper, Jan Steyns, had not only run too near the Southland, contrary to his orders, and in opposition to the protests of the steersmen, and thereby caused that disaster: but had also contemplated deceiving the government by altered and falsified journals, in order to hide as much as possible his indefensible conduct. Whereupon, on the 17th of August, it was determined to indict the said Jan Steyns before the Court of Justice, and he has since been placed under arrest.

The position of the islands against the most outlying

reef of which the *Zeewyk* was wrecked, is shown by the accompanying maps. They lie out of sight of the Southland, and are partly overgrown with some edible wild plants. On them were found not only some excavated wells, but also some signs of a Dutch ship, probably wrecked against the above-mentioned reef, which might have been the *Fortuyn* or *Aagtekerke*, whose crew may have died or perished at sea on their way hither. This also seems to have been the fate of the boat of the *Zeewyk*, which, under the command of the upper-steersman Pieter Langeweg, with eleven common sailors and the papers of the Company, had set out for this port shortly after the wreck of the ship, in order to give information of the mishap and to ask for assistance. Up to this time nothing has been heard of it.

We cannot without painful feelings think of the heavy misfortunes, from which the Company has been a sufferer during the last nine or ten years, especially in the loss of many ships and treasures, which mishaps have to our great concern been considerably increased in number, not only by the disaster which befell the ship *Luchtenberg*, on the Wielingen, on the Zeeland Banks, shortly after leaving port, as communicated to us by the Directors of several Chambers, and particularly by the letter from Amsterdam of the 8th of January; but also by the misfortunes that befell the other ships that had sailed for this country in company with that ship on the 2nd of November, 1727, and were obliged to put into several harbours in a disabled state. Again, by the stranding on the 3rd of July, in Table Bay, of the ships *Middenrack*, *Stabroeck*, and *Haarlem*, of which the *Middenrack* was dashed to pieces and lost all hands, except the few who were on shore at the time, while the two others were driven so close on shore that all hope of safety was abandoned, but succeeded so far as to run their prow aground, whereby the crew and money were saved, and the remainder of the cargo was recovered from the ship undamaged by the sea water. The cargoes of these two stranded ships together with three boxes containing amber from the *Middenrack*, which was washed ashore, have already been brought over by the ships *Meyenberg* and *Nieuwvliet*, they having, through God's blessing, happily ridden through this awful storm from the N.W., not without extreme danger. The ship *Hillegonde* also lost its rudder and gudgeons, and had to be helped into Saldanha Bay. Thus we shall not be able to make use of it here for some time to come, any more than, as we fear, of the ships *Berkenrode* and *Heenhoven*, which had not yet appeared at the Cape on the 18th of July. This is the more alarming, as the *Heenhoven*, on the 9th of February, in the north, at about 57 degrees L., parted through stress of weather from the consorts *Meyenberg* and *Haerbroeck*, in whose company it had left Zeeland on the 24th of January. However we hope soon to welcome the arrival of the above-mentioned two ships, under the blessing of the Most High, who also is besought henceforth to ward off all disasters from the ships and the establishment of the Company, and to make them prosperous in all things; so that the crew of the outward-bound ships may not be afflicted so severely by sickness and death, as has been the case of late with several ships, to such an extent, that it has been necessary to reinforce them one from the other at the Cape; whereby, since the departure of the ship *Meerlust*, in sixteen ships from Holland, only 1375 sailors, 575 soldiers, and 40 artisans, in all 1990 paid servants, including the sick, have come over.

Castle, Batavia, Oct. 30th, 1728.

With ships carrying an average of 200 to 220 people, these figures represent a death roll of from eighty to 100 persons per ship for the outward voyage. No wonder the Governor, Council, and secretary were concerned.

Secretary Hendriks added to his report copies of a letter to the Council of India by Steyns and Nebbens, briefly recounting the events of their voyage, wreck and island sojourn, and the unsigned letter of the skipper in which he complained of mutiny and looting.

We have seen the unsigned note. The signed letter is straightforward and is entirely what would be expected:

161

TO HIS EXCELLENCY, AND THE NOBLE COUNCILLORS OF THE NETHERLANDISH INDIA

We take the liberty of informing you, that, in sailing from the Cape of Good Hope to Batavia with the company's late ship *Zeewyk*, we were wrecked on a reef on the ninth of June, 1727, at seven o'clock in the evening, in the first watch.

The reef against which the vessel struck, is surrounded by a very high and heavy surf, and runs in the shape of a half moon. On the inner side lie many small islands, called Frederick Houtman's Ambrollossen (Abrolhos), which we gained on the eighteenth of June and upon which we remained from that day, until we had fetched from the wreck everything that seemed to us necessary for the preservation of our life, spars, ropes, timber and provisions. As soon as we had got these materials on shore, our carpenter at once set to work with his men, by order of the officers, and by the help of the common people, to build a vessel, so that we might save our lives, if it pleased God. We called it the *Sloepie*, that is, the little sloop, made up from the wreck of the *Zeewyk*. When it was ready for sea, we made sail with a south wind and fair weather on the twenty-sixth of March, having with us the money chests of the company, as well as provisions for the voyage. We continued to enjoy favourable weather throughout the voyage, and so arrived by God's blessing, on the twenty-first of April, 1728, in the Straits of Sunda, eighty-two souls, of whom, we herewith subjoin a list for the information of your nobility and council. We beg to wish you and the council from the bottom of our heart, every prosperity and happiness, and present respectfully our humble services.

Yours etc.

(S.) JAN. STEYNS.

JAN. NOBBENS.

The council were not impressed by the respectful tone of the letter. As reported to the High and Mighty Seventeen, Steyns was arrested by order of the High Court of Justice at Batavia on 17 August 1728. Presumably this was an open arrest and not actual detention, because on 21 September the Attorney General, Jacob Graafland, further requested permission of the Court for "the corporal apprehension of the person of Jan Steyns which was accorded."

On 14 December 1728, Graafland read the claim against the wretched skipper to the assembled Court. Steyns must have trembled when he heard the harsh and exacting terms of the sentence which Graafland demanded.

"In consequence of the malicious and irresponsible mis-sailing of the ship *Zeewyk* by the accused he shall be marched to the place where criminals are usually executed and handed over to the executioner to be tied to a pole and flagellated severely with rods. Forced to labour in chains and without wages for fifteen years at the Company's common works. Remain banished, wherever it pleased the Honourable High Government. And be responsible for the costs of the Court proceedings."

The Court gave sentence in the following year, on 3 May 1729. Gravely the Judges said that it was evident to them that Steyns had, "In an irresponsible way mis-sailed the ship entrusted to him. Moreover he has the impertinence to hand in, on the demand of the late Governor de Haan (he died of sickness during 1728) a counterfeit journal starting with his departure from the Cape, instead of his leaving from Holland. Consequently the accused has committed a notorious falsification."

He was guilty. There was a low murmur of voices in the Court room as the Judges prepared to read the sentence. Many of the *Zeewyk* men were there watching the skipper's face to see how he would take it. Wondering how they would feel in his place. Pity, perhaps, was stirring among them at this moment. When it was read the sentence was not as hard as demanded by Graafland. But nonetheless there was little joy in it for Steyns.

The Court decreed that, "In compensation of losses suffered by the Oost Indische Compagnie in consequence of the irresponsible mis-sailing of the ship *Zeewyk*," Steyns' goods and cash were to be confiscated.

He was to be deposed from office, excluded from his wage,

and declared forever unable to serve the Company in future in any office.

In addition he was to be condemned to be taken to the place where criminal sentences were executed and handed over to the executioner, in order to be exhibited tied to a pole with a board around his neck with FALSIFIER written on it, and to remain there until justice had been done to the other prisoners.

And finally he was to be banished for life from all towns, fortresses, and places under the jurisdiction of the Company without ever being allowed to return to these under penalty of a more severe punishment.

On 3 May, Steyns appealed against his sentence. The High Court of Justice agreed to a revision, and passed a new sentence on 8 August 1729. The terms were exactly the same as the previous sentence. But the Judges decided to excuse him the humiliation of being exhibited with the board, while other prisoners were hanged or flogged according to the seriousness of their misdemeanours.

Three years after gaining command of his fine new ship, Jan Steyns was ruined and disgraced. A criminal in the eyes of the Company. A skipper who had inexcusably lost his ship and many of his men by an act of gross irresponsibility.

He was to be shipped, a prisoner, back to Holland and there released to an uncertain future. The East India Company had such widespread influence that he would never again command a vessel. A marked man for the rest of his days, in an unforgiving world, he would have been lucky to get a job as a common sailor.

His crew fared much better. In their case Jacob Graafland, implacable in hounding to destruction the erring skipper, was as generous as his office allowed. He wrote, in his report of 7 September 1728, that he believed most of the money had been given to the crewmen in Holland for delivery to private persons in the Indies. But it would be difficult to prove this and there was the possibility that men with their own savings would be victimized in any wholesale confiscation. Besides, the crew generally had acquitted themselves well and had salvaged at no small risk the whole of the

Company's treasure. He thought it would be just—with the exception of the disgraced skipper, Steyns, and the merchant, Jan Nebbens—that each man be given back the money found on him and be allowed to keep it, on condition that he would swear that it was his property before the wrecking.

This would reward the gallant seamen of the *Zeewyk* at no expense to the Company, and the private persons who had been smuggling would lose their coin and thus be punished.

The matter came to court on 12 October 1728 and the judgment was pronounced on 3 May 1729—the same day on which Steyns heard numbly of his banishment and disgrace. It followed the lines of Graafland's original suggestion. The Judges decided also to allow one-fourth salvage on money for which no ownership claims were allowable.

Twenty-four sailors heard the judgment with equal satisfaction on 3 May, and during the year (the last on 22 November) another twelve received identical judgments. Steyns and Nebbens failed to win back their ducatons. The court was told that Jan Nebbens had brought in 600 ducatons on behalf of Isaak van Eps, undermerchant for the Cheribon factory; Mattheus Neveling, widower of Hendrina Bernaerds van Breen; and Isaac Plache, citizen of Batavia. They lost the lot. Jan Steyns had also carried 183 ducatons for citizen Plache, and these too were confiscated.

Oddly enough it was as late as 8 June 1729, before Steyns' own money was seized. His nemesis, Graafland, made application for the 556 Rix dollars—a small personal fortune in those times—which Steyns had brought with him. He may as well have left it in the wreck. By edict dated 21 June 1729 it went into the coffers of the East India Company, and he was ruined financially as well as professionally. Sea captains carry grave responsibilities. Even nowadays, the skipper who loses his ship and the lives of crew or passengers by negligence becomes a lonely and disgraced man, shunned by those of his own calling. And since he seldom knows any other trade than the sea, the ruin is more complete than in most other professions.

Poor Steyns. It is hard to find excuses for him, but it is equally difficult not to pity the man at his time of ultimate disaster.

After all, though he had disregarded his sailing orders and wrecked his ship in a way thereby considered unforgivable by his Company, he had made some amends in the aftermath. The salvage of the treasure, the tenacity with which the *Zeewyk* crew had worked under his direction at building the *Sloepie*, and the successful escape from the coast of dead ships and men were surely marks of some credit for the man. But they were never mentioned as such. All the comments in the reports and the Courts were censorious. The East India Company had no forgiveness, and probably he did not expect it. He must have known from the day of the wreck how things would stand with him. The falsified journals, the notes about the mutiny which never was, were the desperation of a man trapped in the web of his fate, and becoming more enmeshed with every pathetic struggle to escape.

He was the substitute skipper. The man who sailed to his professional death because Jan Bogaard, originally chosen for the job, was too sick to command. Chosen at the last moment on a day he must have cursed for the rest of his life.

And the bad luck in the wrecking; the surf sighted too late, the reef in their path after so many leagues of open water. It could have been missed so easily, and yet the *Zeewyk* had been wrecked.

Steyns must have felt like Pelsaert, ruined by that other Abrolhos wreck, the *Batavia*, when he wrote a century earlier, "The pack of all disasters has moulded together and fallen on my neck!" A few months later Pelsaert was dead, his spirit broken.

What happened to Jan Steyns?

Did he rise above his misfortunes and disgrace? Fight back to recapture the respect of his fellows, and a place in the society which had cast him out? Or did he slide into the gutter, crushed by his personal disaster, to die nameless in poverty in a Europe where beggars and the destitute died unnoticed in their thousands every winter?

166

It would be interesting to know whether Steyns did rebuild his life from the shipwreck of his career as they had built *Sloepie* from the wreck of the *Zeewyk*. But we can only surmise. The last official entry is his sentence of 8 August 1729. After that, he disappears.

Of the others, Jan Nebbens, the merchant, went to serve the Honourable Company in the spice trade at Terrate in the Moluccas; the original Spice Islands of history. He signed on for an extra term in the East, and returned to the Company factory at Batavia in 1737. He died there, from one of the many tropical diseases, in February of 1738; ten years after he and the other *Zeewyk* men had reached that port after escaping from the great grim Southland.

Adriaen van der Graeff, the chronicler of the *Zeewyk*, served on a number of Company ships—the *Valkenisse*, the *Berbice*, and finally the *Raedhuys van Vlissingen*, which carried him home to Holland and his wife Elizabeth on 25 November 1729. He signed off, was paid out by the Company in January, 1730, and then he too disappears into history.

The Directors of the Company met in conclave in the Netherlands on 30 August 1729, and the august gentlemen decided that day that the wages of the men who died on the fatal *Zeewyk* voyage would be paid to their heirs. Each man's account of wages was closed at the day of his death.

Pieter Langeweg's account, and those of the men who sailed with him, were never closed, on the one chance in a million that they might turn up one day. With characteristic care, the Company deducted eleven guilders from the money paid to his widow, Maria Dumon, for his sea-chest, which was noted as being five feet long and two feet high. Maria received a final payment of 281 guilders on 30 January 1731. It represented wages due up to 10 July 1727, the day her husband Pieter sailed the *Zeewyk* longboat into the west from the Abrolhos and vanished on the vast ocean. Paid three-and-a-half years later, with the deduction for the oversized chest, it illustrates as clearly as anything else in the *Zeewyk* annals the meanness of spirit of the Company towards its servants.

The story of the ship passed into the legends of the East Indiamen. The survivors were always assured of a good hearing in taverns and fo'c'sles when they told of their ten months lost to the world of men, on the strange coral islands of the Great Southland.

And some were drowned, and some died of the fever, and most from scurvy. A few—very few, for a sailor's life was too hard in those times—of old age. Soon enough they were all in their graves, the century was ended, and the great Vereenigde Oost-Indische Compagnie was dead along with them.

With them died the answer to the mystery of the *Zeewyk*—if, indeed, it was ever known to more than one man.

Why did Jan Steyns, who had nothing to gain from it and all to lose, disobey his orders and take his ship into the forbidden waters of the Southland coast? Risking and losing all?

Why?

15
Lost Guns
and
Silver Dollars

THE INDIAN OCEAN SURF ROLLED AND THUNDERED ON THE outside of the reef, as I stood cradling the elephant tusk in my arms.

The spray smoked from the great crests of the breakers, and drifted on the wind in torn veils. Waist deep in the overfall, I could feel in my legs and hips the power in the surges of the waves washing over the top of the reef.

I stood there deep in thought until the cold made me shiver in the close-fitting rubber suit, and catching a movement out of the corner of my eye I looked down to see sea-worms crawling out of the holes of the riddled green ivory and dropping back in the sea with silent splashes.

Somewhere in the white turbulence of foam beyond the reef, the dead *Zeewyk* lay in her coral shroud of 241 years. Watching the waves break over her I thought of the things which had happened since the *Sloepie* sailed away around the northern horn of the Half Moon Reef, to disappear hull-down on the western horizon.

It was easy to imagine the seals watching the departure

with wary brown eyes, the memory of the bloodstained clubs so fresh that it would be weeks before they would go back to the island beaches. Or the gulls squabbling and fighting noisily over the final food scraps around the warm fire ashes, before the last boatload of men had pulled away from the beach.

The green salt shrubs grew again over the paths and cleared spaces of the camp, and over the mounds of the graves. The tents fell down or blew to ribbons of stained canvas, and the yearly migration of shearwaters alighted and dug the whole island over with new burrows. Cawing and croaking through the nights with their strange cries, flitting low over the bushes like bats in the darkness.

The wreck may have hung together for some seasons. She was strongly built and stubborn. An oak island in the surf, fighting doggedly to retain her identity as a ship while the waves tugged at loose planking, weed grew green up her sides, and guns lay askew in hogged decks. But the day was inevitable when a winter storm would breach her sides, and having forced entry burst her asunder.

The island returned to the state in which the *Zeewyk* men had found it. Pristine; unchanged perhaps over the ten or twenty thousand previous years.

The surf rumbled eternally on the reef. The wind sighed in the dune grasses. Birds, seals, crabs, were born, took their first steps, lived, loved so far as they were able, and died. Out along the reef, coral polyps built their tiny calcium cells, flowered, and reached up for the sun. It was a world in which a thousand years were but a brief passing moment.

Probably the island would have altered little over the next hundred centuries, but in the world outside great changes were taking place. They would have their effect even on the remote rock and coral fastnesses of the Abrolhos.

The Dutch East India Company, whose ships and enterprise caused the accidental discovery of the islands in 1619, and the first human contacts, collapsed in 1794. Bankrupt, despite all the wealth which had passed through its hands. "VOC. . . . Vergaan Ondie Corruptie. . . . Collapsed Under Corruption," said the cynics.

The assertion was partly true. Private trade, the bribes, the concealed thefts, had played their part. But so many of the best men died from fever and scurvy, which bled away strength and initiative. Shareholders demanded dividends even in years when there were no profits, and they had to be paid from capital. The spices, coffee, tea, and textiles which once were Company monopolies were now being grown in other lands. All the factors contributed to a creeping sickness which killed the great company in the end, as the bloody flux and fever had killed its servants in the East.

The once great and glorious VOC died ingloriously, in decrepit old age after a span of 192 years. The world would never see its like again.

There was the sound of bugles and a new national anthem in Europe; the "Marseillaise" of revolutionary France. Drums beat, there was a tramp of marching feet, and the cannon roared flame on fields from Spain to Russia, from Holland to the heel of Italy. Men fell in their tens of thousands, rows of corn before the scythe. In the end, as is usually the way in wars, Death was the main victor. There were many losers. Among them was the Netherlands nation, reduced to a fraction of the wealth and power of a century earlier.

Britain and France, despite their casualties, emerged from the fighting with aggression and ambition unquenched. Two deadly rivals, each mistrustful and afraid of the other. Both with eyes for India, China and the trade of the Eastern seas.

Britain had the advantage of the peace, following the defeat of Napoleon. It was at best an uneasy truce with raw, fresh memories. Among the old wounds, barely healed for Britain, was the damage wrought by French privateers in the mid-Indian Ocean. Under the Tricolour flag, they sallied out from their Mascarene islands base of Ile-de-France like robber sea eagles, capturing $5,000,000 in booty from hapless English East Indiamen in the years 1793 to 1802 alone. When the British won the peace they made certain that they retained the Mascarenes, along with other strategic bases such as the Cape of Good Hope, and changed the name of Ile-de-France to Mauritius to expunge the memory. The unabashed intention was to make the Indian Ocean an English lake, and the British well knew that France could not revive her sea power east of Africa without a base to victual and repair her ships.

When French expeditions showed too much interest in the coast of Western Australia, one of the last great ownerless tracts of land in the world, the British established settlements there as a checkmate. The Union Jack was raised at King George's Sound in 1827, and at Swan River in 1829.

In this way the vast, forbidding territory, which no one had wanted in all the 211 years since its first discovery by the Dutch, which had been variously called Terra Incognita, Eendracht Land, Edel Land, The Southland, New Holland, and on French maps, Terre Napoléon—was finally claimed. Not because the British desired it, but simply to stop anyone else getting it and putting it to troublesome use. It was joined with the settlement at Port Jackson on the east coast under the British crown, and the new name Australia applied to the whole continent. A name more pleasing to the ear than the previous titles, and one which would become permanent in history.

In a surprisingly short time the new settlement at Swan River became a colony, and Western Australia was on the map. The map . . . there was something to consider. . . .

With trade and supply vessels now sailing around Australia from England, India, the eastern Australian penal settlement at Port Jackson, and the cosy little convict hell of Hobart Town, there was a need for accurate charting of the coast. The charts made by Dutchmen a century and a half earlier were historically interesting but hardly satisfactory, as evidenced by the wrecks of their own ships.

It was decided, in 1837, that HMS *Beagle* should work on the survey of Australian waters, and her first task was to fill in the gaps along the Western Australian coast. These included the Abrolhos Islands.

The *Beagle*, a ten-gun brig, was destined for a future place of fame in history. The young naturalist Charles Darwin had travelled aboard during her surveys around the world from 1831 to 1836. The field studies he made—particularly in South America and on the Galapagos Islands—were to inspire his theory of the Evolution of the Species: a conception of life and the relationship of living creatures which would astound and outrage a world brought up on the notion of Adam and Eve.

He was not aboard when she visited the Abrolhos. In some ways it was a pity because coral islands were among his favourite study subjects. He published *The Structure and Distribution of Coral Reefs* in 1842, with a second edition in 1847, and the sea-spawned Abrolhos would have delighted him. He might have quoted them in his hypotheses and made them as scientifically celebrated as the Galapagos. But he had had enough of ships by this time. In his whole five years aboard the *Beagle* he never conquered the queasy green curse of sea-sickness. He had the material he needed. His work from 1836 onwards was in the laboratory, in analyzing the meaning of his volumes of notes and drawings, in writing, and in developing the theory which would one day place him among the most famous and most controversial scientists of his century.

He was still almost unknown in April, 1840, when the *Beagle* dropped her anchors behind the skinny six-mile island where the *Zeewyk* men cut mangrove knees for the *Sloepie*.

They found a wreck on shore, and knew enough of the ancient historical background of the islands to draw an unfortunate conclusion.

"On the south-west point of the island the beams of a large vessel were discovered and as the crew of the *Zeewyk* reported having seen the wreck of a ship on this part there is little doubt that the remains were those of the *Batavia*, Commodore Pelsart, in 1627. We, in consequence, named our temporary anchorage Batavia Road and the whole group of islands Pelsart Group," Lieutenant John Lort Stokes wrote in his journal, which would later become a book, *Discoveries in Australia*, in two volumes. Another *Beagle* lieutenant, Crawford Pasco, also wrote about it in a book *A Roving Commission*, published in 1897.

Their journals give the impression that the *Beagle* men welcomed the chance to display their knowledge of history. They were rather pleased and proud about the Pelsart Group names, though they left the 'e' out of Pelsaert.

But the wreck was not the *Batavia*. Pelsaert's ship, and the bones of the executed mutineers and their victims, lay forty miles to the north. The wreck wood probably came from the *Zeewyk* herself, or the stranger whose fragments were sighted by the *Zeewyk* crew when they landed on the islands.

It was a pity. The *Beagle* men were excellent fellows in every way; courageous, humane, so technically skilled that their maps and charts are used to this day. But on this one point they were in error, and their wrong naming was to throw the history of the area off balance for 123 years. Their names, anomalous today, still remain on the map, but they were more accurate in identifying the *Zeewyk* island.

Stokes wrote, "Captain Wickham and myself landed on the largest island, a quarter of a mile long, forming the north-west extreme of Pelsart Group and which we named Gun Island from our finding on it a brass four-pounder of singular construction." It bore the famous VOC letters, and had a moveable breech-block with a handle. A rare curiosity in days when most cannon were muzzle-loaders with the charge ignited through a touch-hole near the butt. Why did the *Zeewyk* men leave it behind? Perhaps they were overloaded, or maybe it was forgotten in the joyous confusion of the *Sloepie's* departure. A confusion probably aided—if the *Zeewyk* men ran true to character—by the broaching of some more of the liquor cargo in celebration of the opening of the door to escape. They would have been inhuman if there had been no mainbrace spliced, no salute to freedom. The *Beagle* men also found, "Ornamental brasswork for harness on which the gilding was in a wonderful state of preservation, a number of glass bottles and pipes and two Dutch doits (coins) bearing the dates 1707 and 1720. . . . The glass bottles I have mentioned were a stout Dutch build and were placed in rows as if for the purpose of collecting water, and some of them were very large being capable of holding five or six gallons. . . ."

174

They named the deep water pass between the Pelsart Group and the next atoll of islands—which they called the Easter Group from the time of year they arrived—Zeewyk Channel.

Curiously the name Abrolhos was dropped from their chart, and even on the Admiralty chart of today, still based on the *Beagle*'s 1840 surveys, the name for the archipelago is Houtman's Rocks. This is historically annoying because the Dutch had called it Houtman's Abrolhos for 221 years before the visit of HMS *Beagle*, and it was one of Australia's oldest names, dating from 1619. The *Beagle*'s officers themselves spoke of the islands as "Abrolhos" in all their own references to them.

But somewhere, somehow, it was altered to the unromantic Rocks. The new name is inaccurate—they are islands, an archipelago in fact—not mid-ocean lumps or boulders. "Houtman's Archipelago" might have been acceptable, but not "Rocks." The apparent explanation lies in another group of island shoals named Abrolhos off the South American coast. The office of Admiralty hydrographic surveys may have decided that two archipelagos of the same name in different oceans could cause confusion. A navigator might pick up the wrong chart. Though he would be confused indeed if he did not know whether he was sailing the South Atlantic or the Indian Ocean.

Whatever the reason, they are still the Abrolhos to the fishermen, tourists, naturalists, and divers who go there today. Ordinary maps, geography books and atlases also refer to them by their ancient and rightful name, and only the Admiralty remains obdurate with Houtman's Rocks.

The gun found by HMS *Beagle* went to the United Service Museum in London. Many other relics were found as years went by. The crew of the colonial schooner *Champion*, sent in 1848 with a detachment of soldiers to look for treasure from the wreck of the *Ocean Queen*, "found some bones supposed to be those of the mutineers shot by Captain Pelsart," according to the *Inquirer* newspaper of the time. The grisly relics were certainly not those of the *Batavia* butchers. They may have been *Zeewyk* men, the marooned boys, or castaways from other wrecks. The islands were strewn with remains of wrecks.

John Forrest, later to be Lord Forrest, the first Australian peer, found *Zeewyk* pipes and cannonballs while surveying for guano in 1882, on Gun Island.

A guano lease was taken over the island in 1883, by Broadhurst & McNeil, a Geraldton firm. They brought Chinese indentured coolies to dig out the phosphate-rich guano, the bird droppings accumulated in layers feet thick over centuries of healthy seabird digestion. It made marvellous fertilizer for farmers, and there was a world-wide demand. With clinking shovels they cleaned all the top-soil off the island, leaving it a desolate bare rock save for a narrow strip of sand dunes where the *Zeewyk* men had camped on the western side. In the course of their digging they found many relics of the castaways, and one of the partners, Mr Florance Broadhurst, took a great deal of interest in the finds. He had translations made of Dutch documents relating to both the *Batavia* and *Zeewyk*, kept a meticulous list of the relics recovered, and presented most of them in public-spirited fashion to the Western Australian Museum. Like most Western Australians interested in local history he was misled by the report of the HMS *Beagle* survey party, and the names they mistakenly applied. He believed that the *Batavia* had been wrecked in the southern Abrolhos—the incorrectly named Pelsart Group—as did everyone else for the next sixty years or so. He was always hoping something would turn up to pinpoint the scene of the wreck and the infamous mutiny, and went to the trouble of getting a copy of an ancient Dutch work, *Ongeluckige Voyagie van t' Schip Batavia*, "The Unlucky Voyage of the ship Batavia," compiled at Utrecht in 1647 by Jan Jansz, of Amsterdam, mainly from the journals of Francisco Pelsaert. Broadhurst hopefully had a translation made by William Siebenhaar, a Dutch scholar resident in Western Australia, but it contained none of the clues they needed to find the *Batavia*.

There was no question that the material his guano diggers were uncovering on Gun Island came from any other ship

176

but the *Zeewyk*. But if Florance Broadhurst was exasperated by a surfeit of *Zeewyk* relics, and a lack of anything that could positively be identified as coming from the *Batavia*, there is no hint of it in his carefully documented records. In 1897 he supplied the following very complete list of the finds to the Royal Geographical Society of Australasia:

To the Hon. Secretary, Royal Geographical Society of Australasia, Victoria.

Dear Sir,

The following is an accurate list of the relics found on Gun Island of the Houtman Group since our occupation. Articles sent by us to Sir John Forrest, and now in the Perth Museum: 3 large and 24 small cannon balls, 15 flagon-shaped bottles, 1 earthenware jar, 14 rosary beads, 9 lead sinkers, 22 clay pipes and stems, 5 copper fishhooks, 5 knives (much corroded), 6 pieces of lock flint, 7 brass buttons, 5 leaden weights, 16 pistol bullets, 2 copper kettles, 1 glass demijohn, 1 leaden inkpot, 2 coloured tumblers, 1 brass tap, 1 copper pot, 1 copper vessel with cover for padlocking, 1 wine glass, 2 pieces ordnance, 1 silver coin, Phillip IV. of Spain; 3 copper coins, between 1702 and 1724; sundries, including a small piece of copper marked "Zeeland," and two remains of lignum vitae block sheaves; 1 silver coin sent to Wm. Marden, Esq., 14 Fenchurch-street, London, E.C. (A rix-dollar of the city of Utrecht, date 1726.)

In possession of Mrs. G. A. Clifton, Perth: 2 wine glasses of very antique fashion.

In possession of M. Brown, Esq., Geraldton: 1 wine glass, similar to above.

A few copper coins, and sundry of the flagon-shaped bottles, besides a few odds and ends have got into the hands of the public through our employees. They could not be traced or enumerated.

Summary of coins: 18 silver and 48 copper, 2 copper pieces off muskets, one inscribed 'Kamer Zeeland,' the other 'Cameer Zeeland." (Chamber of Zeeland).

A large number of copper articles, comprising fishhooks, manufactured on the spot; roughly made copper dishes

177

for using grease lights in; numerous kinds of buckles, some of which are apparently gilt, more or less; ordinary pins (of copper) with old-fashioned heads; sundry scissors, several spoons and part of spoons; numerous brass buttons; sundry curtain rings; musket fittings; funnel; tap; sea-man's hanger (cutlass) guard; copper parts of blocks and sundry small articles of different kinds, all copper.

A number of iron articles including remains of knives; several cannon balls, two sizes; two shells for ordnance (one of these had still black matter resembling powder in it); chest locks, chest handles, sundry pieces corroded iron.

A number of leaden articles; fishing sinkers; weights; spoon; and upwards of 1,000 pistol bullets of varying sizes.

One pair very fine silver buttons (for officer's cape); legend on them, Joseph escaping from Potiphar's wife. These are just now in London.

Several varieties of work in Lignum vitae wood.

Several lumps of pitch excavated 5 feet deep.

A number of different shaped bottles of various sizes.

Two tobacco boxes with devices.

A number of sundries: clay pipes and stems, broken wine glasses and broken tumblers, fossilized cork, several hundred rosary beads, broken pottery, pieces of slate, bone razor handles and buttons, part of old flint gun lock with undecipherable Dutch inscription; sundry pieces flint.

List of coins found on Gun Island, Houtman's Abrolhos, since January 1, 1894. — Three silver coins about the size of an English half-crown piece; Latin inscription all fairly decipherable. Dates 1633, 1638, 1638, Phillip IV., King of Spain and the Indies (PHIL. IIII., D.G., HISP. ET. INDIAR. REX). The monarch in the centre, this on one side, and on the other a coat of arms with a lion standing on each side, and the inscription, ARCHID. AVST. DVX. BRVG. BRAB.; 1 small silver coin, Dutch, 1657, Frisia; 1 medium-size silver coin, Dutch, 1690, Lat. inscriptions; 1 small silver coin, Dutch, 1709, Hollandia; 1 small silver coin, Dutch,

1722, Zeelandia; 1 small siver coin, Dutch, 1724, Zeelandia; 4 silver coins, dates not decipherable; 37 copper coins, dates from 1702 to 1723, Dutch; 1 British coin, copper, George I., 1720; 1 Chinese coin, which a Chinese merchant in Geraldton tells me belongs to the time of Mon Late, King of China, 835 years ago; 52 coins in all, besides 2 pieces of gun locks marked 'Cameer Zeeland,' and other odds and ends.

Besides the foregoing list, Captain J. Lort Stokes of H.M.S. *Beagle*, discovered a piece of cannon in 1840, and other articles mentioned in Major's "Early Australian Voyages." Surveyor-General S. J. Roe, of Western Australia, also found some articles in the sixties; and finally Sir John Forrest during his visit to the Abrolhos in 1882 made some further finds of clay pipes, etc.

Our own discoveries complete the history of these relics to date.

We trust you will find these particulars useful, and mentioning that press copies of this communication are being furnished by us to the British Consul at Amsterdam and to the Hon. secretary of the Hakluyt Society, British Museum, we remain, Dear Sir,

Yours faithfully,

BROADHURST, MACNEIL AND CO.

One of the tobacco boxes had on its engraved silver lid the picture of a mariner embracing a generously-proportioned lady outside a Dutch tavern and the words:

Eerst t' Gelt Ver Bungt,
En Dan t' Zeegat Uyt
"First the money spend,
Then out of the sea gate." (Back to sea.)

The whole philosophy of an Indiaman sailor in one sentence.

No one, in the years following Florance Broadhurst, has ever been as careful or conscientious in their recording or disposal of relics from Western Australian wrecks. A good deal of assorted material has been found from the *Zeewyk*, and such ships as the 1712 *Zuytdorp*, the 1629 *Batavia*, and

179

the 1656 *Gilt Dragon* through the years, and for the most part has been dissipated.

After being seven-week wonders for their finders, most pieces simply gathered dust on shelves or lay forgotten in cupboards. With deaths, or removals, or the passage of time, their significance was lost. Relics which might have been prized by a museum all too often finished on the junk heap, because no one knew what they were.

Fortunately the Western Australian Museum has acquired a comprehensive collection of Indiamen relics, mainly by private donation. But the loss of the other material is regrettable. It is a pity to lose any part of a historic heritage.

There were so many fragments of ships on the Abrolhos Islands, when the first crayfishermen set up shacks in the Southern Abrolhos after the Second World War to establish a rock lobster export to the United States, that it was hard to tell whether they were bits of Dutch East Indiamen, British brigs, Yankee whalers, or Colonial schooners and horse-transports. The wood lasted well in the salt atmosphere, and pieces of *Zeewyk* were probably burned as fishing camp firewood along with portions of later South Abrolhos wrecks such as the *Ocean Queen* of 1842, *Venus* of 1851, *Cochituate* of 1862, *Marten* of 1878, *Ben Ledi* of 1879, *Eveline Mary* of 1891, and the large sandalwood steamer *Windsor*, wrecked on the Half Moon Reef in 1908. Occasional sticks of weathered sandalwood from her are still burnt today, sending up wafts of aromatic incense smoke originally intended to placate a Chinese joss.

Fishermen who set crayfish pots along the big reef often passed by a group of black cannon lying inside the reef opposite Gun Island. In 1953 Lieutenant Commander M. R. Bromell, commander of HMAS *Mildura*, who was interested in the wrecks and their history, took a party of sailors from the *Mildura* and HMAS *Fremantle* to raise three guns, and brought them back to the Perth Museum. Another gun, shedding flakes of rust and warted sea-growth, was brought in for a tourist festival at Geraldton in 1961, and in 1963 I led an expedition of divers for West Australian Newspapers which recovered some relics and raised another two cannon. It was a pity that any of them were disturbed, though in each case the removal was with the best of intentions. The hard black iron of the guns' casting had been transformed by centuries under the sea into soft brown iron oxide, with no strength or body.

When the guns dried they cracked, split, and fell apart in sheets and slabs of rust. Though a core of a kind remained, it was a mere skeleton of the former gun.

They were handsomer and would have endured much longer, undisturbed on the sea-floor. The guns of Christian Melo. . . .

16
Fate and Fortune

THE GHOSTS LIVED ON IN SEA AND SURGE. . . .

Our *Zeewyk* expedition of 1963 was not what it seemed. We were actually more intent on finding the *Batavia*, which remained undiscovered after 334 years.

A new wreck was like an unclimbed mountain peak. It was important to be the first, and we assumed that the well-known cannon on the reef near Gun Island represented the entire *Zeewyk* wreck. In our eyes there was no prize for being second on the scene, let alone twenty-second.

However, we hoped that the unknown wreck reported by the *Zeewyk* men might prove to be the *Batavia*, and reasoned that, by exploring the area and taking the *Zeewyk* as our starting point, we might find the long-lost command of Francisco Pelsaert.

Two weeks later we retired baffled and disappointed. The *Batavia*, or any other wreck for that matter, was nowhere to be found, and the group of cannon supposed to represent the *Zeewyk* were unsatisfactory. Even allowing for the removals which had taken place we could only account for eight to ten guns. The *Zeewyk* was a 38-gun Indiaman, and her cannon could not roll far or disappear. I believed that this must be a fragment of the wreck which had broken away and washed over the reef carrying a few guns with it. But we failed to prove even that.

We swam in the breakers behind the guns, and for miles along the inside of the reef on either side of them, without finding anything of significance. We took home the two guns we raised, some rosary beads, clay pipes, broken wine glasses, and what may have been a human rib bone from the island. Though the finds created mild public interest we felt we had really achieved very little.

When the *Batavia* was finally found, in June of the same year, she was thirty miles to the north among the outlying cays of the Wallabi Group. One of the finders was Max Cramer, who had been with us on the *Zeewyk* search, and together we joyfully formed an expedition. The discoveries were sensational. We dug up skeletons and sword-chopped skulls on the islands, raised bronze guns with coats-of-arms from the wreck, found navigation instruments, and coins minted before the Spanish Armada. The *Batavia* was every diver's dream of what a wreck should be. Ornamented cannon, blood-thirsty pirates, grinning skeletons, dead men's money, and a moral to adorn the tale with the villains on their gibbets in the end.

The newspapers had a field day, and the *Zeewyk*, seeming drab by comparison, slipped from most people's minds.

But not from mine. There remained a challenge, for I believed, stubbornly, that the main wreck was still to be discovered. It was also true that as divers we thought of wrecks in personal terms, and I felt a certain sympathy for the *Zeewyk* as a Cinderella because she was so overshadowed by the massive *Batavia* epic. But beneath the surface there may have been even stronger reasons. I had read enough of the *Zeewyk* history at that time to have been impressed by the courage and tenacity of her castaways on their coral island, a record of proud qualities which warmed the heart, where the *Batavia* horrors and cruelty made one want to retch and turn away.

I had found the *Batavia* skulls. To this day, the bestial sword-hacks which split the bone stand out in my mind with unwelcome clarity.

Perhaps it was a time when there were too many ugly things in the outside world, and not enough of the stuff of which heroes and ballads are made. A time when my own belief in strength and ideals badly needed supporting.

Whatever the reason, the *Zeewyk* persistently caught at me, and I could not let her alone. I badly wanted to find the main wreck. But in successive years her ghost eluded me. Days of swimming, probing, hoping, in vain until at last I confessed defeat even to myself.

It was only then, and by such blind chance it seemed as though the sea had contrived it all to show who was master, that I found the elephant tusk. Found may be the wrong word—I felt it was thrust upon me, and I have been thoughtful on the matter many times since.

That stroke led to the discovery of the main wreck.

At the time I thought this in itself was the important thing. But I was to learn that it was not. The wreck was a tangible marker, to show that the ship and men had indeed been there alive at one time. But there was more to it all than that.

The living souls of the men, the mother ship *Zeewyk*, and the child *Sloepie*, as well as the spirit of their age, I discovered separately on a symbolic voyage of my own through the journals of the pedant van der Graeff, the letters and records of the Vereenigde Oost-Indische Compagnie, and the pages of many books about the sea and ships I read trying to learn more about the *Zeewyk*.

And there were the islands. . . .

Before finding the wreck, I had always been too busy in a physical way, diving and fishing, and working with boats, to find time for thought and reflection at the Abrolhos. The time we could spend there was restricted, and every day was so precious that we grudged any inactivity.

But spending time in a new experience of solitary exploration with no limit on the days, other than sunrise and sunset, opened a new world. Treading in the footsteps of the

Zeewyk men, with a copy of van der Graeff's journal in one hand, I found the soul of the islands which I had passed by unseeing in my previous haste. In the finding I discovered something more of my own soul. Such is the way of things.

The tusk, the wreck, the journals, the wandering and musing on the islands, led in their turn to this book.

And all these things came from a moment of chance at the Half Moon Reef, the coral Wailing Wall of Jan Steyns, on a March day in 1966.

Fate and fortune.

BIBLIOGRAPHY

CHAPTERS ONE AND TWO

Boxer, C. R. *The Dutch Seaborne Empire* London, 1965
Masselman, G. *The Cradle of Colonialism* Yale, 1963
Zumthor, P. *Daily Life in Rembrandt's Holland* New York, 1963
Vlekke, B. H. M. *The Story of the Dutch East Indies* Harvard, 1946
Zeewyk Papers; Algemeen Ryksarchief, (A.R.A.), The Hague, Netherlands
Minutes and resolutions of Heeren XVIII (ARA Kolonial Archief 267)
Register of Ships Departed from Holland (ARA Kol. Arch. 4390 nr. 64)
Journal of understeersman Adriaen van der Graeff (ARA, VOC archives Zealand series nr. 1691)

CHAPTER THREE

Geyl, P. *Bontekoes East Indian Voyage* Leyden
Parry, J. H. *Europe and a Wider World* London, 1949
Parry, J. H. *The Age of Reconnaissance* London, 1963
Cipolla, C. M. *Guns & Sails In The Early Phase of European Expansion* London, 1965

Mattingly, G. *The Defeat of the Spanish Armada* London, 1959
Williams, G. *Commodore Anson and the Acapulco Galleon* "History Today" magazine, August 1967

CHAPTER FOUR

Boxer, C. R. *The Dutch East Indiamen: Their sailors, their navigators and life on board, 1602-1795.* Annual lecture, 1962, for "The Mariner's Mirror," pub. Vol. 49, No 2, 1963
MacLiesh & Krieger *Fabulous Voyage* London, 1963

CHAPTER FIVE

Marquard, L. *The History of South Africa* London, 1954
Landstrom, B. *The Ship* Netherlands, 1961
Elephant Tusks, ARA Kol. Arch. O.B. Cape of Good Hope 1728 1, fol. 784. Van Riebeeck Society *Kaapse Plakaatboek* and Society Publication No. 25

CHAPTER SIX

Drake-Brockman, H. *Voyage to Disaster* Sydney, 1963
Edwards, H. *Islands of Angry Ghosts* London & New York, 1966
Jansz, J. *Ongeluckige Voyagie van't Schip Batavia* Amsterdam, 1647
Siebenhaar, W. *The Abrolhos Tragedy* Perth *Western Mail*, 1897
Playford, P. E. *The Wreck of the Zuytdorp on the Western Australian Coast in 1712* W.A. Historical Society Journal, 1959
Halls, C. *The Search for the Gilt Dragon* "Westerly" Magazine, Perth, 1964
Francisco Pelsaerts *Batavia* and *Sardam* Journals. ARAKA, VOC 1010, The Hague, Netherlands

CHAPTER SEVEN

Blainey, G. *The Tyranny of Distance* Melbourne, 1966
Clark, C. M. H. *A History of Australia* Melbourne, 1962
Villiers, A. *Captain Cook, The seamen's Seaman* London, 1967
Bligh, W. *The Mutiny on Board H.M.S. "Bounty"* New York, 1962
Sharp, A. *Voyages of Abel Tasman* London, 1968

CHAPTERS EIGHT AND NINE

Fairbridge, Rhodes *Notes on the Geomorphology of the Abrolhos Islands* W.A. Royal Society Journal, 1946-7
Dakin, W. J. *The Percy Sladen Trust Expedition to the Abrolhos*

Islands Linnean Society of New South Wales, 1934

Teichert, C. *Contributions to the Geology of Houtmans Abrolhos* Linnean Society of New South Wales, 1947

Storr, G. M. *The Physiography, Vegetations, and Vertebrate Fauna of the Wallabi Group, Houtman Abrolhos* W.A. Royal Society, 1948

Storr, G. M. *Birds of the Northern Islands of Houtman Abrolhos, Emu* Vol. 65

CHAPTER ELEVEN

Bombard, A. *The Bombard Story* Paris, 1953

Boxer, C. R. *The "Vergulde Draeck"* "History Today" magazine, March, 1968

Schunten *Voyagie* (journal of Abraham Leeman) 1676

Raymond, W. *Silver Dollars of North and South America*

Wilson, S. J. *The Significance of Coins In Identification of Old Dutch Wrecks on the Western Australian Coast* "Numismatic Circular," September 1964

Heeres, J. E. *The Part Borne By the Dutch In the Discovery of Australia* London, 1899

CHAPTERS TWELVE, THIRTEEN, FOURTEEN

Af Chapman, F. *Architectura Navalis Mercatoria* Sweden, 1768

Culver, B. & Grant, G. *Book of Old Ships* London, 1936

Trychare, T. *The Lore of Ships* Adelaide, 1964

Villiers, A. *Monsoon Seas*

Van der Graeff, A. *Zeewyk Journal*

Batavia VOC Papers relating to the *Zeewyk*: ARA Kol. Arch 1974, The Hague, Netherlands

CHAPTER FIFTEEN

Battye, J. S. *Western Australia: A History from Its Discovery to The Inauguration of the Commonwealth* Oxford, 1924

Major, R. H. *Early Voyages to Terra Australia* London, 1859

Stokes, J. Lort *Discoveries In Australia* London, 1846

Pasco, J. Crawford *A Roving Commission* Melbourne, 1897

Uren, M. *Sailormen's Ghosts* Melbourne, 1940

Goldsmith, F. H. *Treasure Lies Buried Here* London, 1946

Edwards, H. *Gods & Little Fishes* London, 1963

Forrest, J. *Report on a Visit to the Abrolhos Islands, 1879* Western Australian State Archives

Broadhurst, F. *Letters & Reports, 1894-97* Western Australian State Archives

INDEX

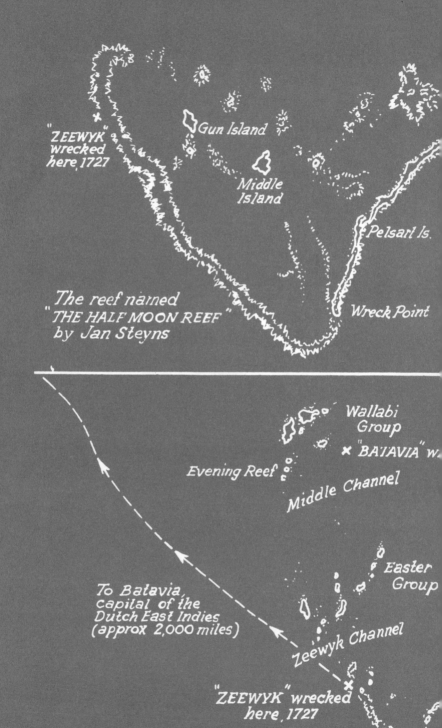

"ZEEWYK" wrecked here, 1727

Gun Island

Middle Island

Pelsart Is.

The reef named "THE HALF MOON REEF" by Jan Steyns

Wreck Point

Wallabi Group

× "BATAVIA" w.

Evening Reef

Middle Channel

Easter Group

To Batavia, capital of the Dutch East Indies (approx 2,000 miles)

Zeewyk Channel

"ZEEWYK" wrecked here, 1727